Introduction

Microwave cookers have been known in the catering industry for many years. Development began after research work into radar during the Second World War, the first microwave cooker being produced in America in the late 1940's. The first domestic model was launched in the mid 1950's and although it has taken many years to prove its worth in the kitchen, it has now been accepted by the housewife as a new concept in cooking and is definitely here to stay as an adjunct to other kitchen appliances. As a compliment to the conventional cooker, refrigerator and freezer, a microwave cooker will make life easier for all those involved in the preparation and cooking of food.

Please read the introductory pages of this book before you begin to use your microwave cooker and you will also find the first section 'Savouries and Snacks' most helpful when taking your first steps in microwave cookery. It may take you a while to 'think microwave' but as you use the microwave more and more you will find that you use your conventional cooker less and less. Although with experience using the microwave will come naturally to you, of course you will need to cook conventionally some foods with which the microwave just cannot cope – Yorkshire pudding, roast potatoes, pancakes, meringues, some pastry and foods that are deep fat fried for example.

This book includes information on heating foods, defrosting, prime cooking as well as some advice on planning the menu to help spread the cooking load when a lot of dishes are required. So whichever model microwave cooker you have chosen, this book has been written as a guide for you and your family to benefit and enjoy their old favourite recipes, as well as many new ones, cooked in a fraction of the time normally spent in meal preparation. We hope you enjoy using your new microwave cooker.

Happy Microwave Cooking!

Contents

Index of Photographs

Selection of fresh fruit, vegetables, meat and fish

Fondue, Mulled Wine

Courgettes Maison, Mushrooms à la Grecque, Creamy Haddock and Sweetcorn, Minestrone Soup, Miniature Meatballs

Chocolate Sauce, Butterscotch Sauce

Selection of Bread and Rolls

Skate with Caper Butter, Scampi Provençale

Roast Turkey, Bread Sauce, Cranberry Sauce, Mince Pies, Christmas Pudding, Traditional Custard Sauce

Liver Pâté, Quick Poor Man's Cassoulet

Stuffed Peppers, German Red Cabbage

Oranges in Caramel, Sponge Pudding, Linzer Torte

Sultana Cake, Chocolate Oaties, Shortbread, Genoese Sponge

Selection of Preserves

Use of the Browning Dish

Double Deckers, Toffee Mallow Crunch, Strawberry Jelly Mousse, Cheeseburgers

Lamb Portugaise, Rice Pudding

Cheesy Spinach Flan, Fruit Cake

Foreword

by Val Collins, Chief Home Economist,
Thorn EMI Domestic Electrical Appliances Limited

At the Tricity and Moffat test and research kitchen, we
have been experimenting with microwave cookers and
discovering their magic for the past 10 years or more.
Who better then, than our team of 6 Home Economists
to put their tried and tested, favourite recipes into a
book to help you, our customers, venture forth into a
new world of Microwave cookery. My sincere thanks go
to all the Home Economists in our team who have
assisted with the compilation of the recipes in this book.

Our thanks also to Bejam Freezer Food Centres Ltd for
supplying some of the food for testing.

The Microwave Cooker

Advantages and Operation

The advantages that the microwave cooker can offer you are
tremendous. Simple to install by plugging it into a 13 amp or 15
amp socket outlet, it can be situated in the kitchen, dining room or
even on a trolley so that it can be wheeled from room to room. The
instruction leaflet supplied with your microwave cooker gives
detailed information on the installation, operation, care and cleaning
of your particular model and should be read through carefully.

With no temperature to set, only timer controls to adjust, the
microwave cooker is so easy to operate that any member of the
family could use it with a stockpile of cooked meals and snacks to be
heated, left for them in the refrigerator or freezer.

Thawing, poaching, baking, roasting, boiling and melting operations
can be carried out in seconds and minutes rather than minutes and
hours with no more effort than it takes to place the food in the oven
and operate the controls. Because food is cooked so quickly, less
valuable nutrients are lost. The cooker is also very economical to use
as all the heat is produced in the food itself and is not wasted
elsewhere. On average up to 75% can be saved on normal cooking
times and up to 50% of your cooking fuel bill. Food can be cooked
and served in one dish so saving on the washing up; and as little
heat is produced in the oven, the kitchen will remain cooler and
cleaner too. In a nutshell, a microwave cooker gives you a more
nutritious meal cooked more quickly using less electricity, and after
the meal there are less dishes to wash up and a cool oven which
cleans with a wipe.

The microwave cooker controls consist mainly of one or two timers,
indicator lights, a start or cook button and a master switch. The
design of these vary between the models, and there are now
available some microwave cookers with touch control. With no

knobs, dials, switches or buttons, the control panel is extremely easy to keep clean and the oven is operated by simply touching the appropriate section of the control panel. The timer is important as all microwave cooking is gauged by time, not time and temperature, and all the timers are marked so that shorter heating or cooking periods can be set with a degree of accuracy. In some models, cooking commences when a start or cook button is pressed, in others when the timer is set. On completion of cooking, an audible warning indicates that the set cooking period is complete and the cooker turns itself off. Alternatively the cooker may be turned off by simply opening the door. Although more expensive to buy, some models incorporate a browning element at the top of the oven cavity which enables microwave cooked food to be browned conventionally. Protection from unnecessary exposure to microwave energy is a requirement of all microwave cookers and interlock microswitches operate when the door is opened, any one of which will turn off the cooker. The cooker can also be turned off by turning the timer back to zero, by turning off the master switch or disconnecting from the electricity supply.

Although we may take delivery of a new kitchen appliance into our homes without too much concern for the technological background, knowing that years of research have ensured that the product will be functional and give satisfactory service, a microwave cooker by these standards is still relatively new and it may be of interest to you to know something of its behaviour.

Microwave Energy

What it is and How it Works

Since early man first accidentally dropped a piece of meat into his open fire and found out that the meat tasted better cooked than raw, the method of applying energy in the form of heat to cook food has hardly changed at all. To cook food placed in a conventional oven, whether it be electric, gas or solid fuel, depends on conduction from the source of the heat to the surface and then the inside of the food. To accelerate cooking in a conventional oven, the source of the heat or oven temperature may be increased but this can cause excessive

browning or overcooking of the outside of the food. Unlike conventional ovens, microwave cookers heat and cook food without applying external heat.

Microwave energy or microwaves are electromagnetic non-ionising, high frequency radio waves, and must not be confused with X rays, Gamma Rays or Ultra Violet Rays which are ionising and are known to cause chemical changes. The worst thing that could happen if one was exposed accidentally to microwaves would be a nasty burn. It would be far more dangerous to sunbathe in the direct glare of the sun for hours on end or subject oneself to a sunlamp.

In the diagram the main components of the microwave cooker are identified.

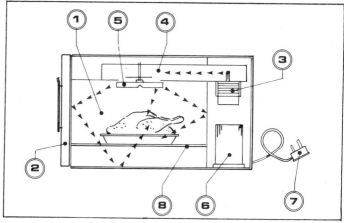

1 The cooking cavity or oven.
2 The opened door.
3 The magnetron.
4 The waveguide.
5 Stirrer blade or fan.
6 The transformer.
7 Flexible power cord and plug top.
8 The oven shelf.

The main function of the transformer is to convert the low voltage of the domestic electrical supply to the high voltages required by the microwave energy generator or magnetron. When microwaves are produced by the magnetron tube, this energy is directed along a waveguide into the oven cavity via the stirrer blade which ensures an even distribution of the microwave energy throughout the oven cavity. However, some models do not incorporate a stirrer blade but depend on a revolving turntable at shelf level in the oven cavity. In these models, food is placed on the turntable and is automatically turned through the microwaves in the oven cavity. Some models incorporate a stirrer blade and turntable which eliminates the necessity to turn or stir dishes during the heating or cooking process.

Microwaves are reflected from some materials such as metal and foil and therefore are also reflected from the metal construction of the oven cavity walls but will pass through such materials as glass, china, pottery, paper and some plastics, all of which make excellent cooking utensils for use in the oven.

tend to align themselves with the energy and thus move rapidly back and forth. This high speed causes friction between the molecules thereby converting the microwave energy into heat to cook the food, quickly and efficiently.

A similar effect can be made by rubbing one's hands together – see how warm they become. We physically experience a similar phenomenon when we stand before a window on a cold, sunny day. The sun generates energy in the form of heat which is radiated through space to the surface of the earth. These rays pass through the glass window without heating it and it feels cold to the touch but the molecules in our body behave like tiny magnets and convert the sun's energy into heat and our body feels warm.

A characteristic of microwave energy is its ability to penetrate food materials to a depth of approximately 2.5 centimetres (1 inch) and produce heat instantaneously and consequently the outer surface of the food may receive more heat than the centre. This is why some recipes will recommend the stirring or turning of foods during cooking and a heat 'equalizing' or 'standing' time is suggested on the completion of some microwave cooking.

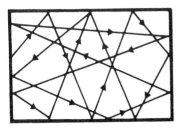

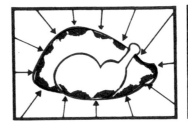

Materials with a high water content, like most foods, absorb microwave energy and the effect on those foods into which the microwaves are absorbed is a rise in temperature. Microwaves vibrate millions of times per second, that is, they have a very high frequency (hence the term microwave). As the electromagnetic waves at a frequency of 2,450 mega Hz enter the food, the molecules

Never operate the microwave cooker when empty. If there is nothing in the oven to absorb the microwave energy, then the microwaves will bounce off the cavity walls and reflect back onto the magnetron thereby shortening its life. A wise precaution would be to leave a cup of water in the oven when it is not in use, just in case it is switched on accidentally.

Getting to Know your Microwave Cooker

Timings

So your microwave cooker has been delivered and now what should you do? The answer to this question is to 'get to know it'. Read the operating instructions supplied by the manufacturer carefully and be prepared to experiment a little, starting off with the most simple dishes.

Try heating a bowl of soup for 3 minutes or so, thaw some bread, cook some baked beans or cheese on toast. In other words, start off 'slowly' and gradually you will get used to cooking times. Be prepared to open the microwave cooker door and have an investigatory look at the food to see how it is cooking just as if you were using a conventional oven. Food is very good tempered and will easily survive the short time the door is open. In fact, heat is produced within the food so quickly again upon door closure that little or no harm will occur even to a light sponge pudding or cake! It is much better to give the dish less time than required and increase the cooking time as necessary than to overcook. Dried out food cannot easily be rectified! Timings in the microwave cooker are important but also very easy once the varying factors which govern the length of cooking time are fully understood.

Power of the Oven

Most microwave cookers have total power inputs of between 1,000 and 1,600 watts with outputs of between 500 and 700 watts respectively. The difference between the input and output power is used by the magnetron, stirrer blade, cooling fan, power converter and the interior and indicator lights.

It is the output power by the magnetron which controls the amount of microwave energy used in the oven cavity and the recipes in this book have been tested on microwave cookers with outputs of 650–700 watts and 500 watts. The instruction leaflet provided with your particular model should give details of the input and output power of the cooker and timings on recipes should be adjusted accordingly.

Cookers with lower outputs will require longer cooking times and these timings are given in brackets in the recipes throughout the book.

Density, Texture and Moisture

Because microwave cooking is so fast, differences in densities, texture and moisture content will show up much more quickly in the end result. You will soon find out that a slice of light textured French or Vienna bread will thaw and heat much more quickly than the sliced, prepacked variety and that a sponge cake will heat through faster than a meat pudding. This is because the lightness in the texture of the food allows the microwave energy to penetrate more easily. Moisture too can affect cooking times as microwave energy reacts mainly on water molecules. Some of the recipes in this book have been adjusted to use more or less liquid than perhaps you are familiar with in order to ensure good cooking results.

Starting Temperatures

Differences in the temperature of the food when placed in the microwave cooker will affect the length of cooking time required. The colder the food, longer heating times will be necessary so allowances must be made when using food directly from the refrigerator or freezer.

Shape

The shape of the food should be as uniform as possible to obtain the best results, but of course this will not always be possible. To protect legs and wings of poultry or the thin ends of fish or a joint such as a leg of lamb from overheating, it is quite in order to wrap them with a small smooth piece of tin foil which will slow down the cooking of these sections of the food. (See 'Suitable and Unsuitable Utensils' page 12). Generally foods which have an overall longer, flatter surface area will heat more quickly than foods which are densely packed into a small dish.

Quantity

As the quantity of food placed into the oven is increased, the length of cooking time needs also to be increased proportionately. For example one jacket potato weighing 100–125g (4–5oz) will take 5–6 mins (7–8 mins), 2 will take 7–9 mins (10–11 mins) and three will take 10–11 mins (12–13 mins) and so on. A rough guide would be to allow approximately between one third and one half extra time when doubling the quantity of food to be heated. Similarly, if you use less than the quantities given in the recipes in this book, then the cooking times must be reduced accordingly.

Utensils

The shape of the dish will affect timings in the microwave, also some utensils will absorb more microwave energy than others. When this happens, as microwaves are being absorbed not only by the food but also to a lesser degree by the material of the dish, then this will affect cooking times. This is explained more fully under the section 'Suitable and Unsuitable Utensils'.

Covering the Food

As when cooking conventionally, lids on dishes or saucepans assist in food heating through more quickly, so it is when cooking in the microwave. Whether a lid on the casserole dish is used or covering food with cling wrap, then steam is trapped inside and this will enable even and slightly faster results to be obtained. Covering food also allows minimal liquid to be used and ensures no flavour loss.

However, when heating through some items, crusty rolls or pastry dishes for example, it would be undesirable to trap the steam as this would prevent a crisp result. In these cases it would be preferable to cover the dish with a piece of kitchen paper towel which would assist in absorbing the moisture given off from the food.

Standing Time

It has already been mentioned that it is better to undercook rather than to overcook the food, giving a little extra time if required. However, foods do continue to carry on cooking after their removal from the oven and some food items will require this standing, resting or 'heat equalization' period to assist with the heating or cooking process. When defrosting (a joint for example), food may begin to cook around the edges before thawing completely in the centre thus a period of standing time in between periods of energy are required to allow more even defrosting. Due to the continuation of the heating or cooking process during the standing time, it is possible to keep foods quite hot whilst further dishes are being cooked in the microwave. This is of course, very useful when preparing a meal. Some dishes, a cake or a pudding for example, should be removed from the oven whilst the top is still slightly moist and left to stand until cooking is complete. Whether food is left to stand inside or outside of the cooker is entirely up to you. It may be that you wish to leave the dish inside the oven out of the way or you may have other foods to cook in the meantime.

Now that you have got to know something about the effects certain factors have upon timing the food items, you will now undoubtedly want to begin to use and cook in your microwave cooker!

Use of your Microwave Cooker

What other piece of equipment is as versatile as the microwave cooker when so many jobs can be carried out so quickly and efficiently? Left over food can be quickly reheated without drying out, even something as small as a tablespoon of baked beans! No longer do you have to remember to take foods out of the freezer the night before when defrosting in a microwave can be carried out in seconds and minutes rather than minutes and hours. Who would think of switching on the conventional oven for heating only one frozen jam doughnut but it can be done in a microwave in just 1–2 minutes, when it will be piping hot! Apart from a few dishes mentioned earlier, a microwave can prime cook foods such as joints, vegetables, fruits, cakes and bread in a fraction of the time and cost normally spent.

Heating Foods

Whether you wish to reheat small portions of left overs, the contents of a can of food or casseroles, the microwave oven will cope with them all without drying and loss of flavour. Dishes can be prepared in advance, refrigerated and then reheated when required, a boon when entertaining. Even the family can heat their own snacks and meals when you are not there.

Foods should be covered where necessary (see 'Covering the food' page 8) which will also help to prevent splashing onto the oven interior. Pastry items and bread can either be covered with, or placed on kitchen paper towels to absorb moisture.

Dishes can be kept warm after heating by covering them with tin foil or simply left in the cooking container during the resting time and therefore it is often quicker to heat or cook food in small amounts rather than to fill the oven with food.

The 'Convenience Food Cooking Chart' on page 35 will give you a guide to timings and resting periods required when heating various food items.

Arrangement of Foods in the Cooker

There may be occasions when you require to heat foods of varying types at the same time, a sponge pudding with a jug of custard, for example. If different heating times are required, then ensure each item is removed from the oven as soon as it is heated. Alternatively the quicker heating food could be 'slowed down' by the careful use of a piece of smooth tin foil (see 'Suitable and Unsuitable Utensils' page 12).

When heating a number of rolls, buns or cakes for example, they should be of equal size where possible and arranged in a circle on a plate or directly on the oven shelf itself.

Plate Meals

You really can cook just once a day if members of the family require meals at different times. Whether just refrigerated to reheat later or frozen to use next week, plate meals are a boon to the busy housewife and ideal standbys for those members of the family who need to cook a meal for themselves when you are not there. And only one plate to wash up!

When arranging food on a plate for reheating, place the food within the well of the plate as evenly as possible, and if thin slices of meat are to be served it is better to place them in the very centre with the gravy poured over and the vegetables around. All items of food on the plate should be at the same temperature and cooked to the same degree to ensure evenness of reheating.

The plate should be covered with cling wrap whilst heating.

The average plate meal (300–400g/12–16oz) will take approximately 2–3 mins (4–5 mins) to reheat from room temperature, 3–4 mins (5–6 mins) from a refrigerator and 5–7 mins (8–9 mins) from frozen. Allow about a minute standing time before uncovering and serving. If you are heating 2 plate meals, one after the other, pop the first one back after the second one has heated, for an extra ½–1 minute to boost the serving temperature.

Turning and Stirring

When food is placed into the oven cavity for heating, defrosting or cooking, microwave energy is directed into the food from all directions including the base of the cavity beneath the glass shelf. Due to the fact however, that microwaves penetrate the food only to a depth of 2.5cm (1in) it is quite likely that the entire outside surfaces of the food will heat through whilst the very centre remains relatively cool. The heating of the centre of the food relies on the conduction of the heat through the food to the centre, therefore the turning of the dishes or the stirring of some foods will be necessary during the heating process. The turning around of dishes is simply giving the dish a quarter turn (90°) or a half turn (180°) on the oven shelf and is stated in the recipes where required. Turning dishes is usually unnecessary in a microwave cooker with a turntable.

When defrosting or cooking certain items, thicker joints of meat or poultry for example, it may be necessary to turn them *OVER* halfway through the cooking cycle.

Stirring food in the dish is simply to ensure that food already heated on the outer edges is pushed to the centre and the unheated centre is pushed to the edges. It is usually quicker to reheat casseroles by stirring rather than to allow heating through conduction to the centre, during a standing or heat equalization period. Alternatively, a suitable up-turned tumbler or cup can be placed in the middle of the dish, thereby eliminating the heating of this very centre section.

Defrosting Food

It is when the microwave cooker is used in conjunction with the freezer that it really comes into its own! When defrosting food by microwave it is so fast compared with normal methods that there is no flavour loss and risk of bacterial growth is minimal by comparison.

Food from the freezer should be placed into a suitable container ensuring that it is large enough to hold the food once it has thawed, particularly important when defrosting sauces, soups, casseroles, etc., and allow sufficient room for stirring the food without spilling.

Commercially frozen foods in foil trays or containers should be removed and placed in another dish. Foods should be covered during the defrosting period where necessary except pastry dishes and bread where kitchen paper towel can be used to absorb moisture (see 'Covering the Food' page 8).

If frozen food was subjected to microwave energy until it was completely defrosted, then the outer edges would begin to cook even before the centre was thawed. To prevent this, frozen food is given bursts of energy with standing times between. If your microwave cooker incorporates a defrost switch or a variable power control dial with a defrost setting, the microwave energy is cycled on and off automatically. This can be done manually where there is no defrost switch or setting, or alternatively a bowl of water can be placed into the oven cavity with the food to be defrosted, thereby slowing down the defrosting process.

The number of heating and resting periods depends on the size or amount of food being defrosted but generally the larger the item, the longer periods of heating and rest are required.

Even with a defrost switch or setting, some food items will still require periods of rest during the defrost cycle, and a final resting period should be allowed before cooking or reheating.

You can check that the food is defrosted by feel and if it needs a little extra time, just put it back into the oven for a little while longer. It is important that joints of meat and poultry are completely thawed and are at an even temperature throughout to ensure good cooking results.

Defrosting and resting times are covered in more detail within the various sections but the 'Convenience Food Cooking Chart' on page 35 deals with smaller items of food and can be used as a general guide.

Cooking Foods

A microwave oven will cook anything in that it will turn food from a raw state into a cooked state. Through experience though we have found that some foods are better for being cooked conventionally. Yorkshire puddings and roast potatoes are good examples and therefore it makes sense if cooking a traditional Sunday lunch to cook the beef, potatoes and Yorkshire pudding in the normal way, leaving the microwave free for the vegetables, sauces, gravy and dessert. Some other dishes for which you will still need your conventional cooker are pancakes, some pastry, meringues and foods which require deep fat frying e.g. fish in batter or breadcrumbs and chips. Frozen chips however, can be thawed in the microwave whilst the fat is being heated conventionally and this will help to shorten the frying time.

A few varieties of potato can be successfully boiled in a roasting bag in the microwave but some are not so good, overcooking on the outside before they are cooked through. Generally it is better to boil peeled potatoes conventionally. Potatoes in their jackets however, can be baked or boiled in the microwave most successfully.

All the different types of food which can be cooked by microwave are given in the various recipe sections. Foods cooked in this way have a fresher flavour and due to the speed of cooking, less valuable nutrients are lost.

Do not think that cooking by microwave means that you must learn completely new cooking techniques. Indeed, most of the basic rules still apply. It is just a case of adapting those rules and yourself to this new method of cooking food.

Seasonings
Salt can have a toughening effect especially on meat and poultry so use minimal seasoning during the cooking process and if in doubt, adjust the seasoning at the finish.

Liquids
In some recipes, the liquid quantities have been altered to suit this method of cooking and may be more or less than you are used to; for example, many vegetables can be cooked with very little water ensuring maximum flavour retention whereas most cake mixtures have to be wetter than normal for a good even rise and moist result.

Timings
The factors which govern timings are given in the section "Getting to Know Your Microwave Cooker". Until you become more experienced check the food frequently, giving it half your estimated cooking time and then allow more time if necessary, remembering that food will carry on cooking for a short time after it has been removed from the oven. If foods begin to 'pop' in the cooker it may be an indication that foods are overheating and that too much time has been allowed.

Appearance of the Food
With experience you will be able to tell if food is cooked by its appearance even although it does not take on the traditional golden brown colour associated with conventionally cooked foods. This can be overcome by garnishing and decorating dishes more attractively. Have available some ready prepared toppings such as browned crumbs, chopped nuts, crushed cereals, brown sugar, apricot glaze, paprika, dried herbs, Parmesan cheese etc. The fact that a cake can be cooked in a few minutes surely outweighs the fact that it is not golden brown in colour when it can be coated with a frosting or dusted with icing sugar.

Some longer cooking joints and poultry will brown to a degree anyway but this can be enhanced by sprinkling with paprika before cooking or the use of gravy brownings or sauces.

If extra browning is required, food can be placed under a hot grill or in a hot oven for a few minutes at the end of the microwave cooking time. This is a way of combining the speed of microwave with the browning acquired by cooking conventionally. Quiches, flans, tarts and filled pancakes are all examples of 'combination' dishes where the 'shells' are cooked in the usual way and then the fillings cooked, set or heated through in the microwave.

The browning of sausages, bacon, chops etc can be carried out in the microwave by the use of a browning dish (See 'Suitable and Unsuitable Utensils' page 12).

Planning the Meal
Complete two, three or four course meals can be cooked in the microwave with a little thought and planning. With experience, you will get more familiar with cooking and standing times. Dishes can be prepared in advance enabling them to be placed back into the oven to be reheated or boost the serving temperature without any harm to the food or loss of flavour.

For many of us, Christmas lunch is possibly the most important meal of the year with family and friends gathered around to enjoy this annual feast. Unfortunately for the housewife it could mean weeks of preparation culminating into days spent slaving in a hot kitchen and missing most of the festivities. With the aid of the microwave though, Christmas lunch need not be a headache at all!

Most food items required for Christmas will freeze for a period of at least 3 months, so by the end of September food can be bought, prepared by microwave and frozen. Many recipes required are contained within the recipe section. Do try the Christmas Pudding recipe which really does save that day of 'steaming the puddings'.

A Few Tips

1 When first planning menus, cook each course separately and gradually progress until a complete meal is cooked by microwave. You will find that organising a time plan will help.

2 As the microwave will not cook roast potatoes successfully, it is possible to roast potatoes and a joint together conventionally, leaving the microwave free for all the other items required.

3 Defrost all foods first except vegetables which can be cooked from frozen. When a lot of vegetables are required, some may be partly cooked then left to stand whilst cooking the rest.

4 When cooking a joint of meat or poultry, vegetables should be cooked during its final standing time.

5 Try to serve one cold course either a starter or sweet which can be prepared by microwave then refrigerated.

6 Soups, casseroles, sauces and gravies may be prepared in advance, placed in serving dishes and then heated when required.

7 Whilst eating one course, the next can be heating or cooking.

8 Where practicable, use cling wrap to cover dishes and roasting bags which can be thrown away afterwards.

9 Line up all the foods to be cooked in the microwave in order and clear the kitchen of any washing up.

10 Have aluminium foil ready to wrap cooked items to keep warm, or if there are a lot of dishes to be served use the warming compartment in your conventional cooker.

Suitable and Unsuitable Utensils

One of the advantages of cooking by microwave is that foods can be cooked in their serving dishes thus cutting down on the amount of washing up. Also owing to the fact that heat is generated within the food, the dishes themselves are generally easier to clean as food tends not to stick.

Microwaves are reflected from metal which means that tin, aluminium, copper and stainless steel cooking utensils cannot be used. However, microwaves pass through glass, china, pottery, wood, straw baskets, paper plates and roasting bags which make them all excellent dishes for use in the microwave cooker, although some pottery absorbs more microwave energy than others and may be less efficient.

There is a test which can be carried out to test the suitability of dishes. Simply place the container in question in the microwave and alongside it a glass of water. After 1½ minutes cooking, the glass of water should be hot and the dish cool. If the reverse is found the dish preferably should not be used. If the water is hot and the dish warm, it would be perfectly in order to use the dish although some efficiency will be lost. Most dishes will remain relatively cool although some heat transfer from the hot food to the dish will occur and the use of ovengloves may therefore be necessary.

Do not use utensils which have been mended with glue as any heat from the food may cause it to melt in the microwave.

Glass

Any type of glass utensil may be used providing there is no metal trim. Thus glass ovenware, e.g. Pyrex, dishes, jugs, casseroles, plates, tumblers and bowls can be used. Ceramic glass dishes such as Pyroflam also respond extremely well to microwave cooking and make attractive serving dishes.

Pottery and China

These can be used in the same way as oven glassware providing there is no metal trim or manufacturer's mark or design in gold or silver. This can cause arcing – blue flashes of light, when the metal trim or pattern will discolour and peel. Some pottery and dark colours can absorb more microwave energy than others which slows down cooking thus making them less efficient. They also may become fairly hot to touch and the use of ovengloves is advisable.

Plastic

Rigid plastic or heat resistant plastic dinnerware may be used but may absorb some microwave energy and will be hotter to touch than other dishes. Freezer containers or lightweight plastic containers can be used for short periods but the heat from food can cause them to melt during prolonged heating. Do not use cream cartons, yoghourt pots or plastic bags as they will melt but the 'boil-in' type bags are excellent although you must remember to prick them to allow steam to escape.

Do not use plastic or plastic freezer bags in the microwave cooker although frozen food wrapped in plastic bags may be placed into the oven for a short period to loosen the package before transferring its contents to another suitable container.

Wood and Straw

Wooden, straw or wicker baskets may be used for short periods when heating dinner rolls for example, but long term exposure to microwave energy may cause them to dry out and distort.

Paper

Many individual servings of food may be heated on serviettes or paper plates. Frozen gateaux, pastries, sandwiches etc. may be placed on paper doyleys before defrosting in the microwave. Kitchen paper towels can also be used to absorb moisture. Greaseproof paper can be used to prevent splashing in the oven by using it to cover food but kitchen paper towel is cheaper. Do not place coloured or patterned kitchen paper towels close to food items as the colour may transfer onto the food.

Wax coated paper cups, plates and paper may be used for short periods only as prolonged heating may cause the wax to melt.

Do not use paper and metal twist ties as they can burn very quickly. Make sure they are removed from plastic freezer bags.

Freezer/Microwave Dishes

There is now a range of freezer/microwave dishes and microwave bakeware on the market specially designed for use in the microwave cooker and most of them give good results. A selection of these would be most useful but would depend on size of family and cooking requirements.

Plastic Spatulas and Wooden Spoons

Plastic spatulas and wooden spoons may be used in the microwave cooker for stirring and mixing. If wooden spoons have absorbed grease or moisture they will become hot.

Cling Wrap

This is excellent for covering dishes and plate meals, although as it is inclined to stretch and dilate during cooking, due to the steam trapped underneath, it is advisable to slit it with a knife or scissors before placing the dish into the microwave cooker. Cling wrap can also be used to line dishes when cooking cakes; the cake can easily be turned out and invariably the dish will not need to be washed.

Roasting Bags

Using roasting bags is an extremely convenient way for cooking a variety of foods ensuring excellent results. They are inclined to enhance the browning of joints and poultry and enable vegetables and fruits to be cooked with very little additional liquid. Do not use the metal ties provided with the bags; elastic bands or string ties can be used instead.

Metal

Metal pots and pans and other utensils with a high proportion of metal must not be used in the microwave. The reason for this is that microwave energy is reflected from metal thus preventing the food within the metal container from cooking and the reflected microwave energy may cause damage to the magnetron. Commercially frozen food in aluminium foil containers should be removed and placed into another dish and never place an unopened can into the oven. Always remove the contents and place into a suitable container.

Metal can be used only in the following instances and as described in specific recipes.

*Aluminium foil
Small smooth pieces may be used to cover bones or narrower ends of poultry, meat or fish for part of the heating or cooking time to prevent overcooking. Care should be taken to ensure the foil is smoothed tightly around the ends. By using aluminium foil in this way you are in fact preventing the microwaves from reaching that area of the food as they are reflected from metal, thus slowing down the heating time. Foil should not be allowed to touch the sides, rear, door or top of the cooker.

*Metal skewers

These may be used if they are placed carefully in large joints. The skewers must not touch one another or the metal sides, rear, door or top of the cooker. Providing these rules are followed, kebab skewers may be used in the microwave but if sparking or arcing occurs, rearrange or remove the skewers.

*Thermometers must not be used with microwave energy unless specially designed. Foods can be removed from the cooker and checked with a conventional thermometer.

*Meat thermometers which are specially designed for use in the microwave cooker are now available and should be used according to the manufacturer's instructions.

Glass Ceramic Browning Dishes or Skillets

These are ceramic dishes with a special coating on the base which is designed to absorb microwave energy. Depending on the size, they are preheated in the microwave for up to 8 minutes then the food to be cooked is placed inside. The hot surface immediately sears the surface of the food – like a grill – while the microwave energy cooks the food. They are excellent for browning steaks, chops, sausages, bacon, chicken portions, etc. For timings see 'Browning Dishes' in the recipe section (page 114).

Use of the Defrost Control or Setting

Where the microwave cooker features a defrost control, when operated, the microwave energy is cycled for so many seconds on and so many seconds off, and so on to allow standing, resting or heat equalization time. The timer will not stop and start but will continue to move while the energy switches on and off in the oven.

Check with your instruction leaflet for the percentage output of the defrost control or setting, as the power level may vary depending on the model.

Generally for defrosting throughout this book reference is made to 50% power level and times will have to be adjusted accordingly for defrosting on higher or lower percentage outputs.

When defrosting frozen foods by cycling the energy, heat is able to penetrate the frozen food by conduction gradually and no surface cooking should take place. The use of small pieces of aluminium foil can be used as described previously to protect the narrower ends of poultry, meat or fish for part of the defrost cycle to prevent any cooking of these thinner parts.

Defrosting using the defrost control or setting may appear to be more complicated than defrosting manually on full (100%) setting when referring to the defrosting instructions given in the various charts throughout the recipe section. You will see on the 'Convenience Food Chart' on page 35 that defrosting certain items using full (100%) setting 2–3 operations are required, whereas using the defrost control or setting, (50%) 4–5 operations are required. These include extra standing times which are in addition to the on and off cycles. We have found these methods are preferable to give a perfect thaw with very little or no overheating of the outside edges. The food is then at an even temperature throughout which ensures that when it is subsequently cooked, a very good result is obtained.

Quicker defrosting is possible by simply placing frozen food into the oven on defrost control or setting until it is completely thawed with one standing period halfway through but less even results are obtained. Alternatively, frozen food can be defrosted until it is warm to touch on the outside edges and then left to stand or heat equalise in room temperature until it is completely thawed.

These defrosting methods are purely a matter of choice, preference or time available and with experience you will be able to determine which method you prefer.

Larger frozen items, joints of meat and poultry for example must be allowed additional standing times when defrosting as indicated in the 'Meat Defrosting Chart' on page 74. Small frozen items like vegetables, cakes, bread rolls, bread slices etc. can be defrosted in a matter of seconds or minutes without using the defrost control.

Heating and Cooking using the Defrost Control

The use of the defrost control is not limited to just defrosting frozen foods. We have found that due to the fact the energy is cycled on and off thus slowing down the cooking time, some food items which benefit from a slower heating can be cooked on this setting:

1 Softening butter, melting method cake mixtures, melting chocolate, combining butter and sugar for caramelizing, melting jellies, melting cheese.

2 Cooking casseroles, either when using tougher cuts of meat or when it is important that seasonings and spices blend well, e.g. curries.

3 Cooking tougher joints of meat.

4 Heating or cooking egg based custards or cream sauces and setting the fillings in pre-baked flan cases, e.g. quiches.

5 Reheating larger casseroles thereby eliminating some of the need to stir as heating of the centre will be through conduction.

6 Cooking larger flatter dishes to prevent the outsides drying out before the centre is cooked, e.g. cheesecake, bread pudding.

7 Poaching larger fruits, e.g. plums, greengages, peaches.

8 Warming bread or rolls in a basket.

9 Proving bread dough.

10 Poaching more delicate fish fillets or cutlets, e.g. salmon.

Whether you use the defrost control for some of the above mentioned items is a matter of choice and time available. We have included some dishes in the recipe section which can be used on defrost control (50%) but if using this setting for heating or cooking, allow double the cooking time given for heating or cooking on full (100%) setting. It is important still to check the food throughout the cooking process and allow extra time if necessary.

Use of the Variable Power Control

The variable power control featured on some microwave cookers enables more flexibility and control of the cooking speed.

Some foods need slower cooking to help tenderise them such as the less expensive cuts of meat and poultry. Slower cooking also allows food flavours to blend thoroughly such as meat sauces and curries.

When a setting other than 'full' (100%) on the variable power control has been selected then the microwave energy into the cooker cycles on and off at varying rates depending on the setting chosen. The timer will not stop and start but will continue to move while the energy switches on and off in the oven. At the lower settings the energy is off longer than the time it is on. As the control is moved onto the higher settings the energy is on longer than the time it is off.

At full (100%) setting, the energy is on all of the time.

Choosing the setting required is rather like choosing the oven temperature on your conventional cooker, the lower the setting or 'temperature', the longer the cooking time and the higher the setting or 'temperature', the shorter the cooking time.

The following guide may be used as an indication of the power levels, in terms of percentage outputs, and their uses. The description of the settings may vary from model to model. It is advisable to check with your instruction leaflet.

10–20%

Use for defrosting joints very slowly and keeping foods warm for about $1/2$ hour or less.

30–40%

As well as defrosting, use for cooking less tender joints and cuts of meat, for softening cream cheese or butter and for slow simmering.

50–60%

Use for faster defrosting and simmering; defrosting and reheating frozen casseroles.

70–80%

Use for reheating left-overs and most precooked foods; roasting joints and to cook foods which contain cheese or cream.

100%

Use for hot beverages and bringing liquids to the boil; melting butter, bacon rashers, fruits and preheating browning dishes.

Most joints of meat and poultry, vegetables and fish can be cooked on this setting. However, many have a better flavour, texture and appearance if one of the slower settings is used when a longer cooking period would be required. The Variable Power Time Chart (page 17) will assist you when calculating the timings required for the different power levels/percentage outputs.

When roasting meat or poultry at a lower setting, best results are obtained by cooking the joint in a roasting bag or covered container and allowing a 10–25 minute standing or heat equalization period halfway through the cooking cycle. If you wish to seal the outside of the meat quickly, then cook the joint at a high setting for the first half of the cooking cycle, allow the standing time, then reduce to a lower setting for the rest of the time. More general information on cooking meat is given in 'Meat and Poultry' in the recipe section.

It is always preferable to use a covered container, roasting bag or boiling bag for reheating or cooking food on the lower settings in order to retain heat and moisture.

We have included some sample recipes under 'Variable Power Control' in the recipe section. This is intended as a guide to help you get the full use of the various settings and will assist you when adapting some of your own favourite recipes.

Do read the previous sections in this book before using the variable power control as all the information given is still applicable.

The Variable Power Time Chart

The timings given in this chart are intended as a guide only as so much depends on the shape, density, texture and temperature of the food. The calculations have been based on a microwave cooker with an average power output of **650 watts** and of course this may vary between different models. Allow slightly extra time if using a microwave cooker with a lower output and slightly less time if using a cooker with a higher output.

Unless otherwise stated, most of the recipes in this book have microwave cooking times given for full when the energy is on 100%. If you wish to slow down the heating or cooking cycle by using one of the lower settings on the variable power control, then this chart will give you the approximate times in minutes for the other percentage outputs. Your instruction leaflet will give the description of the settings/power levels and the percentage outputs of each one on your model.

POWER LEVELS

Minutes Cooking Time	10%	20%	30%	40%	50%	60%	70%	80%	90%	100%
1	10	5	$3^1/_4$	$2^1/_2$	2	$1^3/_4$	$1^1/_2$	$1^1/_4$	1	1
2	20	10	$6^3/_4$	5	4	$3^1/_4$	$2^3/_4$	$2^1/_2$	$2^1/_4$	2
3	30	15	10	$7^1/_2$	6	5	4	$3^3/_4$	$3^1/_4$	3
4	40	20	$13^1/_4$	10	8	$6^3/_4$	$5^1/_4$	5	$4^3/_4$	4
5	50	25	$16^3/_4$	$12^1/_2$	10	$8^1/_4$	$6^3/_4$	$6^1/_4$	$5^1/_2$	5
6	60	30	20	15	12	10	8	$7^1/_2$	$6^1/_2$	6
7	70	35	$23^1/_4$	$17^1/_2$	14	$11^3/_4$	$9^1/_4$	$8^3/_4$	$7^3/_4$	7
8	80	40	$26^3/_4$	20	16	$13^1/_4$	$10^3/_4$	10	9	8
9	90	45	30	$22^1/_2$	18	15	12	$11^1/_4$	10	9
10	100	50	$33^1/_4$	25	20	$16^1/_2$	$13^1/_4$	$12^1/_2$	11	10
20	200	100	$66^1/_2$	50	40	$33^1/_4$	$26^1/_2$	25	22	20
30	300	150	100	75	60	$49^3/_4$	40	$37^1/_2$	33	30

Cleaning and Care

The instruction leaflet supplied with your microwave cooker will give detailed information on the cleaning and care of your particular model and should be read thoroughly.

As most dishes are covered whilst heating, you will notice how clean it is to cook by microwave. With no radiant heat, the oven cavity stays relatively cool during cooking so that any splashes do not burn on and are easy to remove with a warm, soapy or damp cloth. Abrasive cleaning materials of any kind must not be used as they may scratch the interior surface finish. Any splashes which are more difficult to remove can be loosened by placing a container of water into the oven and allowing it to boil for a few minutes. The steam will soften the soilage which can then be wiped away more easily. Afterwards rinse the surfaces and dry with a soft dry cloth or a kitchen paper towel. Any removable tray may be washed in the sink, dried and returned to the oven. It is important that the oven cavity is kept clean for maximum efficiency. Any soilage which is left in the oven will absorb microwave energy thus slowing down cooking times.

The outside of the cabinet should be wiped with a damp cloth, dried and polished with a little spray polish. Ensure that any inlet or outlet air vents are kept clear of tea towels or cloths, etc., during cooking processes.

The door seals must be kept clean and it is advisable to check periodically that the door hinges are not faulty or have become rusty through neglect or lack of service. In the unlikely event of the glass or plastic front panel fracturing, do not use the cooker but contact your service engineer as soon as possible.

Measurements of Ingredients

The quantities for recipes in this book are given in metric and imperial measurement. Exact metric conversions would be difficult to calculate, therefore metric equivalents have been used. Weigh and measure as accurately as possible. Variation in quantity or measurements may mean adjustment in cooking time.

Do not mix metric and Imperial weights in one recipe as all measurements are proportionate.

Mass (weight)

Metric equivalents used	Exact conversions	Imperial
15grams	14.17grams	½oz
25g	28.35g	1oz
50g	56.7g	2oz
100g	113.4g	4oz
200g	226.8g	8oz
300g	340.2g	12oz
400g	453.6g	1lb
1 kilo	907.2g	2lb

Capacity (liquid measures)

25millilitres	28.35ml	1fl oz
50ml	56.7ml	2fl oz
125ml	141.75ml	5fl oz
250ml	283.5ml	½pt
375ml	425.25ml	¾pt
500ml	567ml	1pt
1 litre	992.25ml	1¾pt

Length

2.5centimetres	2.53cm	1in
15cm	15.2cm	6ins
20cm	20.3cm	8ins
25millimetres	25.4mm	1in
150mm	152.4mm	6ins
200mm	203.2mm	8ins

Recipe Section

Points to remember:

1 Read your instruction leaflet and introductory section of this book before starting to use your microwave cooker.

2 Do not use the oven when empty as this could damage the unit. A cup of water left in the unit when not being used for cooking will prevent damage in the event of the oven being switched on accidentally.

3 It is always preferable to undercook rather than overcook the food. Check halfway through the cooking period and adjust time as necessary.

4 The timings given for the recipes are intended as a guide only as much depends on the shape, size and type of utensil used, the temperature of the food at the commencement of cooking and the depth of the food in the dish.

5 Care should be taken when removing dishes from the oven. Some dish materials absorb more microwave energy and may be hot to touch. Heat transfer from foods to the dish may also make dishes hot to touch and the use of oven gloves would be advisable.

6 Deep fat frying must not be attempted as the temperature of the fat cannot be controlled.

7 When thawing frozen foods, remove any closures or ties which contain metal before placing them in the oven.

8 If food begins to 'pop' in the oven, it may be an indication that foods are overheating.

9 Ensure that joints and poultry are completely thawed before cooking.

10 Remember when the amount of food placed in the oven is increased, it is necessary to increase cooking times and these must be adjusted for each type of food.

11 When first using the microwave oven, we would suggest cooking one type of food at a time until you are able to judge the appearance of foods when cooking is completed.

12 After cooking with microwave energy, heat equalisation or standing time is recommended for some food. This allows the distribution of heat evenly throughout the food.

13 Basic principles used to cook food in a conventional oven will also apply to microwave cooking, taking into consideration the short amount of time required to cook foods in the microwave oven.

14 Do not use metal cooking utensils or metal trimmed dishes.

15 The four star freezer symbol shown at the bottom of some recipes indicates that the dish is suitable for freezing: ✱✱✱✱

16 **The cooking times given in the recipes in this book are for microwave cookers with an output of 650–700 watts. For microwave cookers with outputs of 500 watts, the timings are given in brackets.**

Drinks, Snacks and Savouries

This section will help when first using the microwave, starting off with some of the more simple dishes and gradually working towards more complicated ones.

Drinks

Preparing drinks in the microwave is quick and easy. It can even be used to reheat that forgotten half a cup of tea or coffee or refresh left over percolated or filtered ground coffee without any loss of flavour. When making a milky drink in a mug or cup, just heat it until it is at a hot serving temperature; be careful not to let it boil over.

Coffee

Method

1 Blend coffee and sugar with a little of the milk, in a mug. Whisk in the rest of the milk.
2 Heat in the cooker for 1¾ (2¼) minutes, stirring once during cooking. Stir well and serve immediately.

Ingredients per cup
1–2 5ml (tsp) instant coffee
sugar, to taste
150ml (6fl oz) milk

Power Level
Full (100%)

Serves 1

Tea

Method

1 Heat the water in a cup for 2 (2½) minutes.
2 Add the tea bag until tea is the required strength. Remove tea bag and add milk and sugar as required.

Ingredients per cup
150ml (6fl oz) water
1 tea bag

Power Level
Full (100%)

Serves 1

Hot Chocolate

Method

1 Blend drinking chocolate and sugar in a mug with a little of the milk. Whisk in the rest of the milk.
2 Heat in the cooker for 1¾ (2¼) minutes, stirring once during cooking. Stir well and serve immediately.

Variation

Make as above but place a 5–7.5cm (2–3in) cinnamon stick in the mug. Use the cinnamon stick to stir the chocolate.

Ingredients per cup
1 15ml (tbsp) drinking chocolate
sugar, to taste
150ml (6fl oz) milk

Power Level
Full (100%)

Serves 1

Hot Bovril

Method

1 Heat the water in a cup for 2 (2½) minutes.
2 Stir in the Bovril and serve immediately.

Ingredients per cup
150ml (6fl oz) water
1 5ml (tsp) Bovril

Power Level
Full (100%)

Serves 1

Egg Nog

Method

1 Heat the milk in a small jug, in the cooker for 1½ (2) minutes.
2 Beat together the other ingredients. Whisk in the warm milk and serve immediately.

Ingredients per glass
150ml (6fl oz) milk
1 egg
15ml (tbsp) sugar
grated nutmeg or few drops of vanilla essence

Power Level
Full (100%)

Serves 1

Mulled Wine

Method

1 Place the water, sugar and spices in a bowl and heat in the microwave for 4 (5) minutes.
2 Slice the orange and lemon thinly and add to the spiced water. Leave to stand for 10 minutes.
3 Add the wine and reheat for 4 (5) minutes. Strain the wine and heat for 2 (3) minutes.
4 Garnish with extra lemon slices and serve whilst hot.

Ingredients
250ml (½pt) water
100g (4oz) sugar
4 cloves
7.5cm (3in) cinnamon stick
1 orange
1 lemon
1 bottle red wine
few lemon slices

Power Level
Full (100%)

Makes about 1l (1¾pt)

Hot Apricot Cider Cup

Method

1 Heat 250ml (½pt) cider with the cinnamon and almonds in a large bowl for 5 (6) minutes.
2 Liquidise the apricots and juice, or rub through a nylon sieve. Add the apricots to the hot liquid.
3 Add the remaining cider and the tonic. Heat in the microwave for 10–15 (12–18) minutes. Stir well and remove the cinnamon stick before serving.

Ingredients
1l (35fl oz) strong cider
15cm (6 in) cinnamon stick
15g (½oz) blanched almonds
1 822g (1lb 13oz) can apricots
2 241ml (8½fl oz) bottles tonic water

Power Level
Full (100%)

Makes about 1¾l (2¾pt)

Snacks and Savouries

Cooking 'something on toast' is simple with the microwave. Just make the toast conventionally, place it on the serving plate, cover with the prepared topping and cook in the microwave until hot.

Sardines on Toast

Method

1 Remove the bone from the sardines.
2 Butter the slices of toast and pile the sardines on the toast.
3 Garnish each slice with pieces of tomato and heat in the microwave for 30 (60) seconds.

Variations

The following ingredients can be substituted in place of the sardines.
425g (15oz) can baked beans, spaghetti or tomatoes.
200g (8oz) cheese, sliced.
Cook for 3–3½ (4-4½) minutes.

Ingredients

2 120 g (4¼oz) cans sardines
4 slices toast
butter, for spreading
2 tomatoes, sliced

Power Level

Full (100%)

Serves 2–4

Soft Roe Savoury

Method

1 Wash the roe and dry with kitchen paper.
2 Melt the butter in a shallow dish, in the microwave, for 1 (1½) minutes.
3 Add the roe, cover with a lid or cling film and cook for 1½ (2) minutes.
4 Turn the roe and cook for a further 1 (1½) minutes. Season and add chopped parsley and lemon juice.
5 Serve on hot buttered toast.

Ingredients

12 soft herring roes (about 100g/4oz)
25g (1oz) butter
salt, black pepper
chopped parsley
few drops of lemon juice
1 slice hot buttered toast

Power Level

Full (100%)

Serves 1

Sautéed Kidneys on Toast

Method

1 Remove and discard the skin and cores from the kidneys. Chop finely and toss in the seasoned flour.
2 Melt the butter in a shallow dish for 1 (1½) minutes. Add the onion and cook for 1½ (2) minutes.
3 Add the kidneys, stir, cover and cook for 4½ (5) minutes, stirring once during cooking.
4 Adjust seasoning and serve on hot buttered toast.

Ingredients

4 lambs kidneys
2 15 ml (tbsp) flour
25g (1oz) butter
1 small onion, finely chopped
seasoning
2 slices hot buttered toast

Power Level

Full (100%)

Serves 1 or 2

Individual Cheese Soufflés

Method

1 Place the butter in a bowl and melt for 1 (1½) minutes.
2 Stir in the flour and gradually blend in the milk. Cook for 1½ (2) minutes until thickened, stirring every 30 seconds. Add the cheese.
3 Beat in the egg yolks into the mixture one at a time and season.
4 Stiffly beat the egg whites, fold into the mixture and divide between 8 individual soufflé dishes or ramekin dishes.
5 Cook 4 at a time for 1–1½ (1½–2) minutes. Serve immediately, sprinkled with a little paprika pepper.

Ingredients

25g (1oz) butter
15g (½oz) flour
125ml (¼pt) milk
75g (3oz) cheese, finely grated
3 eggs, separated
seasoning
paprika pepper

Power Level

Full (100%)

Serves 8

Tuna Stuffed Rolls

Method
1 Slice the tops from the rolls, remove the centres from the rolls and crumb.
2 Melt the butter in a bowl for 1 (1½) minutes, add the breadcrumbs, tuna fish, cheese and seasoning. Mix well together and heat through for 1–1½ (1½–2) minutes.
3 Fill the rolls with the mixture, replace tops and heat through for 1–1½ (1½–2) minutes.
4 Serve straight away.

Ingredients
4 crispy rolls
25g (1oz) butter
198g (7oz) can tuna fish, flaked
50g (2oz) cheese, finely grated
seasoning

Power Level
Full (100%)

Serves 4

Spanish Omelette

Method
1 Place the vegetables and tomato in a shallow dish with the oil. Cover with cling wrap and cook on full (100%) for 1½–2 (2–2½) minutes.
2 Whisk the eggs and seasoning together and pour over the vegetables. Cook uncovered on 50% setting for 8 (10) minutes.
3 Leave to stand for 1 minute.
4 Do not fold the omelette but serve on a warm plate with a green salad.

Ingredients
100g (4oz) frozen mixed vegetables
1 tomato chopped
1 15ml (tbsp) oil
4 eggs
seasoning

Power Level
Full (100%) and 50%

Serves 2

Bacon Sandwich

Method

1. Remove rind from bacon. Snip fat to prevent curling. Put rashers on a plate and cover with kitchen paper.
2. Cook for 1 (1½) minutes, ½ turn and cook for 2 (2½) minutes.
3. Make up the sandwich, dipping the bread in the melted bacon fat. Place the sandwich on a plate and cover with cling film.
4. Heat in the cooker for 30 (45) seconds, cut and serve.

Note

A frozen ready made up sandwich can be placed on a plate and covered as above. Cook for 1½ (2) minutes and then serve.

Ingredients
3 rashers bacon
2 slices bread

Power Level
Full (100%)

Serves 1

Quick Crumpet Pizzas

Method

Heat the crumpets in the microwave for ½–1½ (2–2½) minutes, depending on the number.

Lightly butter the crumpet. Place the ham on the crumpet and top with tomato, herbs, seasoning, onion and grated cheese.

Cook as follows:
1 crumpet – 1 (1½) minutes
2 crumpets – 1½ (2) minutes   or until the cheese
4 crumpets – 2½ (3) minutes   is melted.

Garnish with sliced green olives.

Ingredients for each pizza
1 crumpet
knob of butter
½ slice cooked ham
2 thin slices tomato
pinch of mixed herbs
salt and pepper
few onion rings
15–25g (½–1oz) cheese, grated
sliced green olives

Power Level
Full (100%)

Stuffed Baked Potatoes

Method

1 Scrub the potatoes, cut a slit along the top of each one and cook in the microwave for about 10–12 (12–15) minutes.
2 Remove the soft potato from the skins and mix it with the other ingredients, reserving a little of the cheese.
3 Pile the mixture back into the potato skins. Sprinkle the tops with the reserved cheese and cook for a further 2 (3) minutes before serving.

Ingredients

2 potatoes (each 225–250g/9–10oz)
25g (1oz) butter
50g (2oz) cheddar cheese, grated
1 15ml (tbsp) milk
salt and pepper

Power Level

Full (100%)

Serves 1–2

Garlic Bread

Method

1 Cut the loaf into slices 2–2.5cm (¾–1in) thick, cutting not quite through to the bottom of the loaf.
2 Beat the butter well. Add the other ingredients and mix thoroughly.
3 Spread a large knob of the butter in each of the cuts in the loaf.
4 Protect the thin ends of the loaf with small pieces of aluminium foil. Place the loaf on kitchen paper on the glass shelf of the cooker and cover with pieces of damp kitchen paper.
5 Cook for 1½ (2) minutes or until the butter has melted.

Variation

To make Herb Bread substitute
1 15ml (tbsp) fresh mixed herbs, finely chopped
or
1½ 5ml (tsp) dried mixed herbs in place of the garlic and parsley.
Cook as above.

Ingredients

1 short, crusty French stick
125–150g (5–6oz) butter, softened
3–4 cloves garlic, crushed or finely chopped
or
1–1½ 5ml (tsp) garlic granules
1 5ml (tsp) parsley, chopped

Power Level

Full (100%)

Bacon and Onion Flan

Method

Place onion in a small bowl, sprinkle with salt, cover with cling film and cook for 2 (3) minutes.

Place bacon on kitchen paper in the cooker and continue cooking, with the onion, for 1 (1½) minutes. Arrange onion and bacon in flan case.

Beat the eggs with the salt and pepper and add the milk. Place the pastry case on kitchen paper, on the cooker shelf and pour the egg mixture over the bacon and onion.

Cook for 2 minutes, ¼ turn, stand for 1 minute. Cook for 1 minute, ¼ turn, stand for 1 minute. Repeat the last operation until the flan is set in the centre. Approximately 4 or 5 times. Serve hot or cold.

Note

If using 50% setting cook as follows: Cook for 6–8 (8–10) minutes, ½ turn, stand for 5 minutes, cook for 6–8 (8–10) minutes.

Ingredients

1 onion, finely chopped
2 rashers bacon, chopped
17.5cm (7in) pre-cooked pastry flan case
2 eggs
salt and pepper
100ml (4fl oz) milk

Power Level

Full (100%) or 50%

Serves 3–4

Sausage and Mash

Method

Place the potato in a small bowl. Heat the water in the microwave for 3 (4) minutes. Pour over the potato.

Whilst the potato is standing cook the sausages. Prick them well, then cover with kitchen paper. Cook for 4–5 (6–8) minutes, turning once.

Reheat potato for 1 (1½) minutes and serve.

Ingredients

1 65g (2½oz) medium-sized packet instant potato
250ml (½pt) water
4 large sausages

Power Level

Full (100%)

Serves 2

29

Eggs

When 'frying' or poaching eggs in the microwave, prick the yolks with a sharp pointed knife otherwise steam build up may cause them to explode; for the same reason never boil eggs in their shells in the microwave except by the method given in this section. Be careful not to overcook scrambled eggs as they may become rubbery in texture.

The cooking times given for eggs are intended as a guide as much depends on how well done one likes them but remember to remove them from the oven just before they are set as they will carry on cooking for a short while afterwards. Leave them to stand for a minute before serving but if they are not quite set sufficiently for your liking, return them to the oven for a further 10–15 seconds.

Boiled Eggs

Method
1 Wrap the eggs tightly in a piece of *smooth* foil to reflect the microwaves, thus preventing the eggs from exploding.
2 Place the water in a bowl and add the eggs. Cover with cling wrap and cook for 3 (4) minutes. Stand for 2 minutes. Drain and unwrap the eggs then serve.

Ingredients
4 eggs
375ml (¾pt) boiling water

Power Level
Full (100%)

Serves 2–4

Note
Whilst the recipe does not save any cooking time, it is the only method by which eggs can be boiled in the microwave.

Poached Eggs

Method

1 Place boiling water in a large, shallow dish. Break the eggs into the hot water.
2 Cover and cook for 1½ (2½) minutes, drain the eggs then serve on hot buttered toast.

Note

Eggs may be placed in individual cups or ramekin dishes. Pierce the yolks and add a small knob of butter, if required, to each one and cook for 1¾ (2) minutes. Turn dishes halfway through cooking time if necessary.

Ingredients

500ml (1pt) boiling salted water
4 eggs
4 slices hot buttered toast

Power Level

Full (100%)

Serves 2 or 4

Fried Eggs

Method

1 Melt the fat in a shallow dish for 30 (45) seconds. Break the eggs into the hot butter and pierce the yolks.
2 Cover and cook for 30 (45) seconds. Stand for 1 minute then give dish ½ turn and cook for 15–30 (45–60) seconds.

Ingredients

15g (½oz) butter or margarine
2 eggs

Power Level

Full (100%)

Serves 1 or 2

Scrambled Eggs

Method

1 Beat the eggs, milk and salt together.
2 Melt the butter in a bowl for 1 (1½) minutes. Pour in the egg mixture and cook for 1 (1½) minutes.
3 Stir well and cook for 2–2½ (2½–3) minutes, stirring every 30 seconds. Serve with hot buttered toast.

Ingredients

4 eggs
4 15 ml (tbsp) milk
pinch of salt
25g (1oz) butter
2 slices hot buttered toast

Power Level

Full (100%)

Serves 2

31

Egg and Bacon

Method

1 Lay the bacon in a shallow dish, cover with kitchen paper and cook for 1 (1½) minutes.
2 Remove the bacon and add the egg. Pierce the yolk, cover and cook for 30 (45) seconds.
3 Stand for 1 minute, return the bacon to the dish and cook, still covered, for 15–30 (30–45) seconds.

Ingredients

2 rashers bacon
1 egg

Power Level

Full (100%)

Serves 1

Herb Omelette

Method

1 Melt the butter in 20cm (8in) shallow dish for 30 (45) seconds. Mix all the other ingredients together in a separate bowl.
2 Brush the melted butter around the base and sides of the dish. Pour in the egg mixture and cover with cling film.
3 Cook for 1 (1½) minutes, stir well, cook for 1 (1½) minutes. Uncover and cook for 1 (1½) minutes. Turn out of the dish and serve immediately.

Variation

The following ingredients can be substituted in place of the herbs. Cook as above.
2 15ml (tbsp) cheese, grated
2 15ml (tbsp) cooked ham, chopped
2 15ml (tbsp) cooked onion, chopped

Ingredients

15g (½oz) butter
4 eggs
2 15ml (tbsp) milk
salt and pepper
1 15ml (tbsp) mixed dried herbs

Power Level

Full (100%)

Serves 1–2

Cheese

Cheese melts very quickly in the microwave so remove cheese dishes from the oven just as the cheese is softened; if overcooked cheese becomes leathery.

Macaroni Cheese

Method

1 Place macaroni in a large, shallow dish. Pour over the boiling water and stir in the oil and salt. Cook for 10 (14) minutes then separate with a fork.

2 Place onion and a pinch of salt in a roasting bag and cook for 3 (4) minutes.

3 Melt the butter in a bowl for 1 (1½) minutes. Blend in the flour and gradually stir in the milk. Cook for 5–6 (7–8) minutes, stirring every minute. Beat in the egg yolk, cheese, seasoning and cooked onion.

4 Pour the sauce over the macaroni and garnish with the sliced tomato. Cook for 3 (4) minutes and serve immediately.

Ingredients

100g (4oz) macaroni
250ml (½pt) boiling water
1 15ml (tbsp) oil
1 5ml (tsp) salt
1 small onion, chopped
pinch of salt
25g (1oz) butter
25g (1oz) plain flour
375ml (¾pt) milk
1 egg yolk
75g (3oz) cheddar cheese, grated
1 tomato, sliced

Power Level

Full (100%)

* *******

Serves 3–4

Welsh Rarebit

Method

1 Place all ingredients for the filling in a small bowl and melt in the cooker for 30 (60) seconds. Stir well.

2 Spoon onto the slices of toast and cook for 15 (30) seconds. Serve immediately.

Ingredients

100g (4oz) Cheddar cheese, grated
25g (1oz) butter
1 5ml (tsp) dry mustard
1 15ml (tbsp) brown ale
salt and pepper
2 slices toast

Power Level

Full (100%)

Serves 1–2

Fondue

Method

1 Rub the garlic round the inside of a heatproof dish. Place the cheese, seasonings, wine and lemon juice in the dish.
2 Melt the cheese in the microwave for 4–5 (6–7) minutes. (The cheese and wine will not combine).
3 Blend the cornflour with the Kirsch, add to the fondue, stir and cook for 1–2 (2–3) minutes until slightly thickened.
4 Serve with crusty bread, keeping fondue warm over a spirit lamp or dish warmer.

Note

The fondue can be cooked as follows: Melt the cheese mixture on 50% setting for 10 (12) minutes, add the blended cornflour and Kirsch then cook on 50% setting for 6 (7½) minutes.

Ingredients

1 clove garlic, crushed
100g (4oz) Gruyère cheese, grated
100g (4oz) Emmenthal cheese, grated
black pepper and grated nutmeg
125–175ml (5–7fl oz) dry white wine
squeeze of lemon juice
2 5ml (tsp) cornflour
1 liqueur glass Kirsch

Power Level

Full (100%) or 50%

Serves 4

Swiss Toast

Method

1 Butter the toast, put a slice of ham on each and cover with a slice of cheese.
2 Cook one at a time for 1 (1½) minutes.
3 Serve with scrambled egg.

Ingredients

4 slices toast
butter
4 slices cooked ham
4 slices Swiss cheese

Power Level

Full (100%)

Serves 4

The Convenience Food Chart

This chart gives information on thawing and cooking commercially frozen foods as well as heating some canned and packet foods. Before defrosting frozen food items, please read section 'Use of the Defrost Control or Setting', for those microwave cookers with a defrost control or setting facility.

Food and Quantity	Method	Defrosting Instructions on 'Full' (100%)	Defrosting Instructions on 50% setting	Cooking Instructions on 'Full' (100%)	Special Points
MEAT AND MEAT PRODUCTS					
Gravy and roast beef, frozen 113g (4oz)	Remove from the foil dish and place on a serving plate.	Cook for 2 (3) minutes Stand for 2 minutes	Cook for 2 (3) minutes Stand for 2 minutes Cook for 3 (4) minutes Stand for 2 minutes	Cook for 1½ (2) minutes	Lightly butter the rim of the serving plate. Any gravy splashes from defrosting and cooking will then wipe off easily before serving.
Gravy and roast beef, frozen 340g (12oz)	Remove from the foil dish and place on a serving plate.	Cook for 3 (4) minutes Stand for 3 minutes	Cook for 5 (6) minutes Stand for 5 minutes Cook for 5 (6) minutes Stand for 9 minutes	Cook for 3½ (5) minutes	
4 Beefburgers, frozen	Place on kitchen paper on the glass shelf.			Cook for 3–4 (5–6) minutes, turning over once.	
Individual meat pie, frozen 100g (4oz)	Remove from the foil dish and place on a serving plate.	Cook for 1½ (2) minutes Stand for 2 minutes	Cook for 2 (3) minutes Stand for 2 minutes Cook for 2 (3) minutes Stand for 3 minutes	Cook for 1–1½ (1½–2) minutes Turn Cook for 1–1½ (1½–2) minutes	Brush the pies with milk after thawing.
Family sized meat pie, frozen 400g (1lb)	Remove from the foil dish and place on a serving plate.	Cook for 2½ (3½) minutes Stand for 5 minutes Repeat this once	Cook for 5 (7) minutes Stand for 10 minutes Cook for 2 (3) minutes Stand for 2 minutes	Cook for 3 (4) minutes Stand for 4 minutes Turn Cook for 3 (4) minutes Stand for 4 minutes	
Shepherds pie, frozen 454g (16oz)	Remove from the foil dish and place on a serving plate.	Cook for 5 (7) minutes Stand for 2 minutes	Cook for 6 (7½) minutes Stand for 6 minutes Cook for 3 (4) minutes Stand for 6 minutes	Cook for 5 (6) minutes	Cover the plate with cling film to prevent drying out.

Food and Quantity	Method	Defrosting Instructions on 'Full' (100%)	Defrosting Instructions on 50% setting	Cooking Instructions on 'Full' (100%)	Special Points
Lasagne, frozen 454g (16oz)	Remove from the foil dish and place on a serving plate.	Cook for 4 (5) minutes Stand for 3 minutes Cook for 3 (4) minutes	Cook for 8 (10) minutes Stand for 6 minutes Cook for 4–5 (6–7) minutes	Cook for 9 (12) minutes	Cover the plate with cling film to prevent drying out.
Individual steak and kidney puddings, frozen 125g (5oz)	Remove from the foil dish and place on a serving plate.	Cook for 2 (3) minutes Stand for 5 minutes	Cook for 2 (3) minutes Stand for 5 minutes Cook for 3 (4) minutes Stand for 2 minutes	Cook for 2½ (3½) minutes Stand for 2 minutes	
Individual meals 'Boil in Bag', frozen 170g (6oz)	Slit bag and place on a serving plate.	Cook for 2 (3) minutes Stand for 2 minutes	Cook for 4 (5) minutes Stand for 6 minutes	Cook for 1½ (2½) minutes	
Individual meals 'Boil in Bag', frozen 227g (8oz)	Slit bag and place on a serving plate.	Cook for 2 (3) minutes Stand for 2 minutes	Cook for 4 (5) minutes Stand for 6 minutes Cook for 2 (3) minutes Stand for 2 minutes	Cook for 2½ (3½) minutes	
Individual meals 'Boil in Bag with rice', frozen 227g (8oz)	Follow thawing instructions then place rice in a ring on a serving plate. Pour sauce into centre and follow cooking instructions.	**Rice** – cook in dish of boiling, salted water for 4 (6) minutes. Stand for 5 minutes **Sauce** – Slit bag and cook for 2 (3) minutes Stand for 2 minutes	**Rice** – cook on 'Full' **Sauce** – slit bag and cook for 4 (5½) minutes Stand for 6 minutes	Cook for 4 (5) minutes Stir sauce	Cover plate with cling film to prevent drying out during cooking.
4 Beefburgers, canned 283g (10oz)	Remove fat from the beefburgers and place on kitchen paper or a plate.			Cook for 2 (3) minutes Turn over Cook for 2 (3) minutes	The kitchen paper absorbs the excess fat during cooking.
Large steak and kidney pudding, canned 440g (15½oz)	Remove from the tin with a palette knife. Place in a small bowl.			Cook for 4–5 (6–7) minutes Stand for 5 minutes	The small bowl will help the pudding to keep its shape during cooking although it may collapse slightly.
Soya protein chunks, canned 425g (15oz)	Place soya in a bowl.			Cook for 4 (5) minutes	Stir once during cooking.
Soya protein mince, canned 425g (15oz)	Place soya in a bowl.			Cook for 3 (4) minutes	Stir once during cooking.
FISH 2 Cod steaks, frozen 200g (8oz)	Place the steaks on a plate	Cook for 3½ (4½) minutes Stand for 5 minutes	Cook for 3 (4) minutes Stand for 6 minutes Cook for 3 (4) minutes Stand for 6 minutes	Cook for 3 (4) minutes Turn if necessary	Cover the plate with cling film to prevent drying out during cooking.

Food and Quantity	Method	Defrosting Instructions on 'Full' (100%)	Defrosting Instructions on 50% setting	Cooking Instructions on 'Full' (100%)	Special Points
Buttered, smoked haddock 'Boil in Bag', frozen 198g (7oz)	Slit the top of the bag.			Cook for 6 (8) minutes	
10 Fish fingers, frozen	Place in a circle on a plate.	Cook for 4 (5) minutes Stand for 2 minutes	Cook for 6 (7) minutes Stand for 4 minutes	Cook 1½ (2½) minutes, turn if necessary. Cook 1 (2) minutes	Dot fish fingers with butter before cooking.
Fish steak in sauce 'Boil in Bag', frozen 170g (6oz)	Slit bag before cooking.	Cook for 2½ (3½) minutes Stand for 2 minutes	Cook for 4 (5) minutes Stand for 4 minutes Cook for 3 (4) minutes Stand for 5 minutes	Cook for 1½ (2½) minutes	

CANNED AND FROZEN SNACKS

Food and Quantity	Method	Defrosting Instructions on 'Full' (100%)	Defrosting Instructions on 50% setting	Cooking Instructions on 'Full' (100%)	Special Points
Pizza, frozen 283g (10oz)	Place on serving plate.			Cook for 5 (7) minutes	Turn once during cooking.
Soup, canned 250ml (½pt)	Pour into a mug.			Cook for 3 (4) minutes	Stir once during cooking.
Pasta dishes, canned eg. macaroni cheese 425g (15oz)	Place in a bowl or on a serving plate.			Cook for 4½ (5½) minutes	Stir twice during cooking.
Spaghetti in tomato sauce, canned 440g (15½oz)	Place in a bowl or on a serving plate.			Cook for 3 (4) minutes	Stir once during cooking.
Baked beans, canned 220g (7¾oz)	Place in a bowl, on a plate or on toast.			Cook for 1½ (2) minutes	Stir once during cooking.
Baked beans, canned 425g (15oz)	Place in a bowl, on a plate or on toast.			Cook for 3½ (4½) minutes	Stir once during cooking.
Baked beans and beefburgers, canned 425g (15oz)	Place in a bowl or on a plate			Cook for 4½ (5½) minutes	Stir twice during cooking.
Garden peas, canned 425g (15oz)	Place in a bowl.			Cook for 4½ (5½) minutes	Stir twice during cooking.
Milk puddings and custards, canned 440g (15½oz)	Place in a bowl or serving jug.			Cook for 3 (4) minutes	Stir once during cooking.
Sponge pudding, canned 298g (10½oz)	Place on a plate or in a bowl.			Cook for 2 (3) minutes	Turn once during cooking.

Food and Quantity	Method	Defrosting Instructions on 'Full' (100%)	Defrosting Instructions on 50% setting	Cooking Instructions on 'Full' (100%)	Special Points
FROZEN CAKES AND BREAD					
1 Slice of homemade cake	Place on a plate.	Cook for ¾–1¼ (1–2) minutes	Cook for 1½–2 (2–2½) minutes		The time needed varies with the size and type of cake.
Cream sponge 225–250g (9–10oz)	Place on a serving plate.	Cook for 15 (15–30) seconds Stand for 3 minutes	Cook for 1 (1½) minutes Stand for 4 minutes		Times give are sufficient to thaw the sponge. The cream may still be hard in the centre of the cake but further heating will melt the cream.
Cream doughnuts	Place on kitchen paper or a plate.	**1 doughnut** Cook for 15 (30) seconds Stand for 2 minutes **4 doughnuts** Cook for 30–45 (45–60) seconds Stand for 2 minutes	**1 doughnut** Cook for 30 (45) seconds Stand for 4 minutes **4 doughnuts** Cook for 1¼ (2) minutes Stand for 5 minutes		
Jam doughnuts	Place on kitchen paper or a plate.	**1 doughnut** Cook for ¾–1 (1–1¼) minutes Stand for 2 minutes **4 doughnuts** Cook for 2–2½ (2½–3) minutes Stand for 2 minutes	**1 doughnut** Cook for 1½ (2) minutes Stand for 2 minutes **4 doughnuts** Cook for 4 (5) minutes Stand for 4 minutes		
1 Mince Pie	Place on kitchen paper or a plate.	Cook for 15–30 (30–45) seconds	Cook for 30–45 (45–60) seconds	Cook for 15–30 (30–45) seconds	
4 Mince Pies		Cook for ½–1 (1–1¼) minutes	Cook for 1–1¼ (1¼–1½) minutes	Cook for 30–45 (45–60) seconds	
Cheesecake with fruit topping	Place on a plate.	Cook for 2 (2½) minutes Stand for 5 minutes Cook for 1 (1½) minutes Stand for 5 minutes	Cook for 4 (5) minutes Stand for 5 minutes Cook for 2 (2½) minutes Stand for 5 minutes		
Bread dough for a 400g (1lb) loaf	Place on kitchen paper.	Cook for 2½ (3½) minutes Stand for 5 minutes Cook for 1½ (2) minutes Stand for 5 minutes	Cook for 5 (6) minutes Stand for 8 minutes Cook for 3 (4) minutes Stand for 5 minutes	**Proving** Cook for 15 (15–30) seconds Stand for 5 minutes Repeat this 3–4 times **Cooking** Cook for 5–6 (7–8) minutes	

Food and Quantity	Method	Defrosting Instructions on 'Full' (100%)	Defrosting Instructions on 50% setting	Cooking Instructions on 'Full' (100%)	Special Points
1 Slice of bread	Place on the glass shelf.	Cook for ½–1 (¾–1¼) minutes	Cook for 1–1½ (1½–1¾) minutes		The time needed varies with the size and thickness of the slice.
1 Large loaf of bread	Place on the glass shelf.	Cook for 2 (3) minutes Stand for 6 minutes Cook for 2 (3) minutes	Cook for 4 (5) minutes Stand for 12 minutes Cook for 5 (6) minutes Stand for 4 minutes		Wrap the loaf in cling wrap to prevent drying out.
MISCELLANEOUS Butter, frozen 250g (8.8oz)	Place the butter in a bowl.	Cook for 15–30 (30–45) seconds Stand for 30 seconds Cook for 15 (30) seconds Stand for 30 seconds	Cook for 30–45 (45–60) seconds Stand for 1 minute Cook for 30 (45) seconds Stand for 1 minute		Butter wrapped in paper can be placed directly on the glass shelf but a foil wrapper should be removed.
Porridge (1 serving)	Place 4 15ml (tbsp) porridge oats in a bowl. Add 125ml (¼pt) milk (or milk and water mixed) and a pinch of salt. Mix well.			Cook for 1¾ (2½) minutes Stand for 1–2 minutes	Stir twice during cooking. Serve with milk and demerara sugar.
Jelly 135g (4¾oz)	Place the jelly in a bowl or measuring jug.			Cook for 15–30 (30–45) seconds	Break the jelly into small cubes before melting.
Chocolate 100g (4oz)	Place the chocolate in a small bowl.			Cook for 1 (2) minutes	Break the chocolate into small pieces. Beat well after melting.
Blanched almonds 50g (2oz)	Place the whole or halved almonds onto a flat dish or plate or into a boiling or roasting bag.			Cook for 6 (7–8) minutes or until required 'toasted' colour	Stir or shake frequently.
Desiccated coconut 50g (2oz)	Place coconut onto a flat dish or plate or into a boiling or roasting bag.			Cook for 10 (12) minutes or until required 'toasted' colour	Stir or shake frequently.
Chestnuts 10–12	Place chestnuts onto a flat dish or plate, slit skins			Cook for 1–1½ (2–2½) minutes until hot and soft	Shell, and use as required.

Starters

Included in this section is a selection of different starters as well as some more usual ones. They make good appetizers to a meal but some may also be used for supper dishes. Those which are to be served cold can be prepared in advance and refrigerated; those which are to be served hot can also be preprepared but can be quickly reheated when you and your guests are ready.

Spicy Apple Juice

Method

1 Place apples, water and sugar in a roasting bag and cook in the microwave for 5 (8) minutes.

2 Liquidise the apples with the white wine and a generous pinch of cinnamon.

3 Stir in the cider and serve.

Ingredients

400g (1lb) cooking apples
2 15ml (tbsp) water
sugar, to taste
generous pinch of cinnamon
125ml (¼pt) white wine
250ml (½pt) cider

Power Level

Full (100%)

Makes 625ml (1¼pt)

Courgettes Maison

Method

1 Trim and wash the courgettes. Place in a large dish, cover with cling wrap and cook for 4–5 (6–7) minutes. Rinse in cold water.

2 If using frozen prawns, heat in a covered dish for 2½ (3) minutes to thaw.

3 Remove a thin strip from the top of each courgette, cutting lengthways and reserving the strips. Scoop out and chop the flesh of each courgette.

4 Melt the butter, in a bowl, for 1 (1½) minutes. Add the onion and courgette flesh and cook for 2 (3) minutes, add the tomatoes, paprika and seasoning and cook for a further 2 (3) minutes.

5 Stir the prawns into the mixture. Fill each courgette case and top with the reserved strips of courgette.

6 Cover the dish with a lid or with cling film and cook for 3–4 (5–6) minutes.

7 Mix the cheese and white sauce together and season to taste. Pour the sauce over the courgettes and reheat, uncovered, for 2–3 (3–4) minutes.

Note: Alternatively, the courgettes can be reheated more slowly for 5 (7) minutes on 50% setting.

Ingredients

8 small courgettes
200g (8oz) shelled prawns
25g (1oz) butter
1 onion, finely chopped
4 tomatoes, skinned, deseeded and chopped
1 5ml (tsp) paprika
salt and pepper
250ml (½pt) white sauce (see page 56)
50g (2oz) grated Parmesan cheese

Power Level

Full (100%) or 50%

Serves 4

Eggs en Cocotte

Method

1 Mix the cream with the seasonings, to taste. Whip the mixture lightly until the cream is thick but not stiff.
2 Divide the butter between 4 ramekin or individual soufflé dishes and melt for 30 (60) seconds. Brush the butter around the dishes and break an egg into each dish.
3 Pierce the yolk of each egg then spoon over the cream mixture.
4 Cover and cook for 1 (1½) minutes, turn and leave for 1 minute. Cook for 30 (60) seconds.
5 Sprinkle with more paprika and garnish with parsley before serving.

Note: Alternatively, the dish can be cooked on 50% setting as follows: cook for 2–2½ (3–3½) minutes, stand for 1 minute. This helps prevent over-cooking of the yolks and cream.

Ingredients

125ml (¼pt) double cream
salt and pepper
garlic salt
paprika pepper
25g (1oz) butter
4 eggs
4 sprigs parsley, for garnish

Power Level

Full (100%) or 50%

Serves 4

Miniature Meatballs

Method

1 Prepare garlic butter by blending the butter, onion, garlic, parsley and pepper thoroughly. Cover and chill until hard.
2 Place the onion in a large bowl and cook for 1½ (2) minutes. Add the other ingredients and mix thoroughly.
3 Shape about 1 15ml (tbsp) meat mixture around ¼ 5ml (tsp) of garlic butter, sealing in the butter completely.
4 Place the meatballs in a single layer in the serving dish 12–18 at a time. Cook, uncovered for 3 (5) minutes, turn dish, cook for 2 (4) minutes.
5 Garnish with extra chopped parsley, before serving.

Ingredients

100g (4oz) butter, softened
1 15 ml (tbsp) onion, finely chopped
3 cloves garlic, finely chopped
2 15ml (tbsp) chopped parsley
pinch of pepper
1 onion, finely chopped
400g (1lb) minced beef
50g (2oz) breadcrumbs
salt and pepper
1 egg, beaten
1 15ml (tbsp) tomato purée
1 5ml (tsp) Worcestershire sauce

Power Level

Full (100%)

Makes about 40

42

Creamy Haddock and Sweetcorn

Method

1 Cook and mash the potatoes or make up the instant potato. Mix in a large knob of butter and the parsley. Using a large rosette pipe, pipe a border of potato onto 4 scallop shells.

2 Place butter, flour and milk in a bowl. Cook for 1 (1½) minutes, beat thoroughly, cook for 1 (1½) minutes. Repeat this operation until the sauce thickens (approximately 3 times).

3 Add the fish and corn to the sauce and season to taste. Cook for 1 (1½) minutes, stir, cook for 1 (1½) minutes. Add the cream, correct the seasoning and spoon the mixture into the scallop shells.

4 Heat the scallops for 4–5 (6–7) minutes. Sprinkle with paprika and serve immediately.

Ingredients

400g (1lb) potatoes or 1 medium-sized packet instant potato
knob of butter
1 15ml (tbsp) chopped parsley
20g (¾oz) butter
20g (¾oz) plain flour
150ml (6fl oz) milk
200g (8oz) haddock, cooked and flaked
50g (2oz) frozen sweetcorn
salt and pepper
2 15ml (tbsp) single cream
paprika pepper

Power Level

Full (100%)

✱✱✱✱

Serves 4

Salmon Stuffed Pancakes

Method

1 Stir the salmon, mustard and onion into the white sauce. Season to taste.

2 Spread an equal amount of sauce on each pancake and roll up. Lay the pancakes in a shallow serving dish and moisten with the lemon juice.

3 Cover the dish with cling wrap and cook in the microwave for 8 (10) minutes, giving ¼ turn every 2 minutes.

4 Top with soured cream and sprinkle with the chopped chives. Serve immediately.

Ingredients

1 198g (7oz) can salmon, drained and flaked
1 5ml (tsp) mustard
1 15ml (tbsp) onion, finely chopped
250ml (½pt) white sauce (see page 56)
salt and pepper
8 20cm (8in) cooked pancakes
2 15ml (tbsp) lemon juice
125ml (¼pt) soured cream
2 15ml (tbsp) chopped chives

Power Level

Full (100%)

Serves 4–8

Mushroom Stuffed Cannelloni

Method

1 Heat 2 15ml (tbsp) of the oil in a bowl for 2 (2½) minutes. Add the onion and garlic and cook for 2 (2½) minutes. Add the sliced mushrooms, herbs and seasoning and cook for 3 (4) minutes.

2 Add the tomatoes to the mixture and adjust the seasoning if necessary.

3 Cook the cannelloni in a large covered bowl of boiling salted water with the other 1 15ml (tbsp) of oil, for 5–6 (7–8) minutes. Drain the pasta and rinse with cold water, separating the tubes.

4 Fill the cannelloni with the mushroom mixture and place in a serving dish.

5 Season the white sauce with the basil, paprika and salt. Add the Parmesan cheese and mix thoroughly.

6 Pour the sauce over the cannelloni and cook for 3–4 (5–6) minutes. Sprinkle with paprika before serving.

Ingredients

3 15ml (tbsp) oil
1 onion, finely chopped
2 cloves garlic, finely chopped
100g (4oz) button mushrooms, sliced
1 5ml (tsp) sweet basil
salt and pepper
4 tomatoes, skinned and chopped
8 cannelloni tubes
250ml (½pt) white sauce (see page 56)
½ 5ml (tsp) basil
½ 5ml (tsp) paprika
salt
25g (1oz) Parmesan cheese

Power Level

Full (100%)

Serves 4

Mushrooms à la Grecque

Method

1 Melt the butter in a large dish for 1 (1½) minutes, add the onion and garlic and cook, covered, for 2 (2½) minutes.

2 Wash and coarsley chop the mushrooms. Skin and deseed the tomatoes, roughly chop. Add mushrooms and tomatoes to the onion and cook for a further 3 (4) minutes.

3 Stir the tomato purée into the wine and then add the liquid to the mixture. Cook for 2½ (4) minutes.

4 Add half the parsley and pepper to taste. Leave to cool, then chill for 2 hours.
Add the rest of the parsley and serve.

Ingredients

25g (1oz) butter
1 small onion, finely chopped
1 clove garlic, crushed
400g (1lb) button mushrooms
4 firm tomatoes
1 15ml (tbsp) tomato purée
1 wine glass white wine
2 15ml (tbsp) parsley, chopped
pepper, to taste

Power Level

Full (100%)

Serves 6–8

Potted Shrimps

Method

1 Put the shrimps in a bowl, cover and heat in the microwave for 30 (60) seconds. Stand for 1 minute then heat for 1 (1½) minutes.
2 Place about 125g (5oz) of butter in a bowl and melt for 3 (4½) minutes. Liquidise the shrimps, melted butter and seasonings to give a smooth paste.
3 Press mixture firmly into a small dish and chill for ½ hour.
4 Melt the remaining butter for 2 (3) minutes. Smooth the top of the shrimp mixture and pour over the rest of the butter. Cover and refrigerate until needed.

Ingredients

200g (8oz) frozen shrimps
200g (8oz) unsalted or clarified butter
½ 5ml (tsp) dried basil
pepper to taste

Power Level

Full (100%)

Serves 4

Devil's Dip

Method

1 Melt the butter in a bowl in the microwave for 1 (1½) minutes. Stir in the flour and curry powder and gradually add the milk.
2 Cook for 3 (4½) minutes, stirring every minute.
3 Add the remaining ingredients, leaving the cream until last. Stir well and serve hot or chilled.

Ingredients

25g (1oz) butter
3 15ml (tbsp) plain flour
½ 5ml (tsp) curry powder
250ml (½pt) milk
1 green pepper, deseeded and chopped
50g (2oz) walnuts, chopped
50g (2oz) raisins
2 15ml (tbsp) wine vinegar
1 15ml (tbsp) lemon juice
pinch of cayenne pepper
125ml (¼pt) double cream

Power Level

Full (100%)

Serves 4

Mediterranean Stuffed Aubergines

Method

1 Trim the aubergines. Cut into 8 thick slices, sprinkle with salt and heat in the microwave for 3 (4) minutes. Leave to stand for 10–15 minutes. Wash thoroughly in cold water.

2 Remove the centre of the aubergines and reserve. Place the aubergine rings in an ovenware serving dish.

3 Heat the oil in a mixing bowl for 2 (2½) minutes. Add the onion, pepper and garlic and cook for 3 (4) minutes. Add the meat and cook for 4 (6) minutes.

4 Chop the reserved aubergine centres and stir into the meat mixture, along with the rest of the ingredients. Cover the bowl with cling wrap and cook for 5 (6) minutes, stand for 5 minutes.

5 Cook the aubergine rings, in the serving dish, for 4–5 (5–6) minutes. Stuff the rings with the filling. Cover the dish with cling wrap and cook for 3 (4) minutes. Sprinkle with Parmesan cheese before serving.

Ingredients

2 medium-sized aubergines
2 15ml (tbsp) oil
1 onion, finely chopped
½ green pepper, finely chopped
2 cloves garlic, finely chopped
200g (8oz) mince
4 tomatoes, skinned and chopped
1 courgette, trimmed, halved and thinly sliced
2 15ml (tbsp) tomato purée
1 5ml (tsp) oregano
salt and black pepper
Parmesan cheese

Power Level

Full (100%)

✳✳✳✳

Serves 4–6

Hot Cinnamon Grapefruit

Method

1 Halve the grapefruit, remove the pips and loosen around the flesh of the fruit. Place each half grapefruit in an individual bowl.

2 Mix the cinnamon and sugar together. If using the spirit, pour 1 15ml (tbsp) over each half grapefruit, then sprinkle with the sugar mixture. Place half a glacé cherry in the centre of each half grapefruit.

3 Heat the grapefruit in the microwave for 1 (1½) minutes, turn, heat for 1 (1½) minutes. Serve immediately.

Ingredients

1 large grapefruit
pinch of cinnamon
25g (1oz) demerara sugar
2 15ml (tbsp) sherry or rum (optional)
1 glacé cherry

Power Level

Full (100%)

Serves 2

Pasta Salad

Method

1. Place water, salt and oil in a large bowl and heat in the cooker for 4 (5) minutes. Add the pasta and cook for 10 (12) minutes. Stir well, then drain and rinse with cold water.
2. Return the pasta to a serving bowl and stir in walnuts and raisins.
3. Peel the carrot and dice, chop the apple, removing the core. Add carrot and apple to the salad.
4. Drain the kidney beans and rinse if necessary. Finally add beans and dressing to the salad and toss lightly before serving.

Ingredients

500ml (1pt) water
1 5ml (tsp) salt
1 15ml (tbsp) oil
100g (4oz) shell pasta
50g (2oz) walnuts, chopped
50g (2oz) raisins
2 carrots
1 green eating apple
1 425g (15oz) can kidney beans
oil and vinegar salad dressing

Power Level
Full (100%)

Serves 6–8

Quick Kipper Pâté

Method

1. Slit the kipper bag. Heat the kippers for 2 (3) minutes, stand for 5 minutes.
2. Cook the kippers for 3 (5) minutes. Skin the fillets and flake the fish. Place in a liquidiser goblet, with the yoghurt. Liquidise until well mixed.
3. Cook the onion in a small, covered, dish for 1 (2) minutes then add to the kipper mixture. Add the other ingredients, seasoning to taste.
4. Pack the mixture into a serving dish and garnish with parsley. Cover and chill in the refrigerator for at least an hour before serving. Serve with hot buttered toast.

Ingredients

1 170g (6oz) pkt frozen kipper fillets
100ml (4fl oz) natural yoghurt
1 small onion, chopped
salt and pepper
squeeze of lemon juice
1 15ml (tbsp) chopped parsley
sprigs of parsley for garnish
buttered toast

Power Level
Full (100%)

✳✳✳✳

Serves 4

Soups

Whether used as a starter to a meal or as a snack, home made soups are nourishing and quickly prepared in the microwave. Try the 'Chicken and Sweetcorn' recipe – it's delicious!

If reheating canned soups and every member of the family likes different sorts, well why not! Simply heat a bowl or mug of canned soup in the microwave for about 3 (4) minutes, two bowls or mugs will take about 5 (8) minutes.

Packet soup should be emptied into a large jug or bowl, the recommended amount of cold water added and then left to stand for 20–30 minutes to allow the ingredients to soften. Bring to the boil in the microwave, about 8–10 (12–14) minutes depending on quantity. Cook for half the time recommended on the packet and then leave to stand for the remaining half before serving.

Cream of Cucumber

Method

Place the onion in a large shallow dish, pour over the boiling stock, cover and cook for 5 (8) minutes.

Peel the cucumber and cut into pieces. Add to the stock with the fresh or dried mint. Cook, still covered, for 30 (35) minutes.

Liquidise or sieve the soup, return it to the bowl. Blend the arrowroot with the cream, add to the soup and reheat until soup thickens slightly.

Adjust seasoning, colour lightly and chill thoroughly before serving. Garnish with diced cucumber or chopped mint.

Note

The soup can be reheated on 50% setting to prevent overheating of the cream.

Ingredients

1 onion, sliced
750ml (1½pt) boiling stock
1 large cucumber
1 sprig mint or generous pinch of dried mint
2 5ml (tsp) arrowroot
65ml (2½fl oz) single cream
salt and pepper
green food colouring

Power Level

Full (100%) or 50%

Serves 4–6

Cream of Vegetable

Method

Place the stock in a large bowl and add the vegetables. Cook for 10 (12) minutes then liquidise.

Melt the butter in a dish for 1 (1½) minutes. Add the other ingredients and the vegetable purée.

Cook for 10 (12) minutes, stirring once during cooking. Remove bouquet garni, adjust seasoning and serve.

Ingredients

500ml (1pt) chicken stock
½ onion, chopped
2 carrots, diced
100g (4oz) peas
75g–100g (3–4oz) cauliflower florets
25g (1oz) butter
25g (1oz) plain flour
250ml (½pt) milk
salt and pepper
bouquet garni

Power Level

Full (100%)

Serves 4–6

Bortsch

Method

1 Place the onion, carrot, herbs and seasoning in a large dish with the stock. Cook for 5 (7) minutes.
2 Add the beetroot and cook for 10 (12) minutes. Liquidise and strain the soup, return it to the bowl.
3 Stir in the cream and serve.

Note

If the soup is to be frozen the cream should not be added until reheated ready for serving.

Ingredients

1 onion, finely chopped
1 large carrot, chopped
2–3 sprigs parsley
1 bay leaf
salt and pepper
1l (1¾pt) chicken stock
400g (1lb) cooked beetroot, chopped
125ml (¼pt) soured cream

Power Level
Full (100%)

Serves 4–6

Mushroom

Method

1 Slice the mushrooms, reserving 6–8 slices for garnish. Cook these in milk for 1 (1½) minutes.
2 Melt 25g (1oz) butter for 2 (2½) minutes. Toss the onion in the butter and cook for 2 (2½) minutes. Add the mushrooms, stock and bouquet garni and cook for 20 (25) minutes.
3 Remove the bouquet garni and sieve or liquidise the soup.
4 Melt the remaining butter, in a large, shallow dish, for 2 (2½) minutes. Combine butter with flour and milk then add the mushroom purée. Heat through for 10 (12) minutes, stirring once.
5 Season to taste and garnish with the sliced mushrooms.

Ingredients

200g (8oz) button mushrooms
50g (2oz) butter
½ onion, chopped
375ml (¾pt) boiling stock
bouquet garni
25g (1oz) plain flour
500ml (1pt) milk
salt and pepper

Power Level
Full (100%)

Serves 4–6

Tomato

Method

Cook the bacon in a large, covered dish for 2 (3) minutes, add the chopped vegetables and cook for 5 (7) minutes.

Blend the cornflour with a little stock then add with the rest of the boiling stock, the bouquet garni and the peppercorns. Cover and cook for 25 (30) minutes. Remove bouquet garni.

Pass soup through a sieve or liquidise and return to the dish. Add the sugar, seasoning and cream. Serve with croûtons.

Note

If the soup is to be frozen the cream should not be added until reheating, ready for serving.

Ingredients

100g (4oz) diced bacon
1 stick celery, chopped
400g (1lb) tomatoes, skinned and chopped
1 carrot, chopped
25g (1oz) cornflour
750ml (1½pt) boiling stock
bouquet garni
6 peppercorns
pinch of sugar
salt and pepper
1 15ml (tbsp) cream

Power Level

Full (100%)

Serves 3–4

Chicken and Sweetcorn

Method

Heat the oil in a large bowl for 2 (2½) minutes. Add the onion and celery and cook for 3 (4) minutes.

Add the boiling stock, sweetcorn and seasonings and cook for 5 (6) minutes.

Add the chicken and cook for 2 (2½) minutes. Cool slightly and add the dried milk, then liquidise.

Heat the soup for 2 (2½) minutes. Toss in the almonds and serve immediately.

Note

If the soup is to be frozen, do not add the almonds until reheating, ready for serving.

Ingredients

1 15ml (tbsp) oil
1 onion, chopped
1 stick celery, chopped
500ml (1pt) boiling chicken stock
200g (8oz) frozen sweetcorn
salt and pepper
100g (4oz) cooked chicken, diced
50g (2oz) dried milk
25g (1oz) flaked almonds

Power Level

Full (100%)

Serves 3–4

Minestrone

Method

1 Melt the butter, in a large bowl, for 1 (1½) minutes. Add carrot, onion, leek, celery and garlic and cook for 3 (5) minutes.
2 Add stock, pasta, rice, salt and pepper. Cook for 5 (7) minutes.
3 Add tomatoes and baked beans and cook for 5 (6) minutes.
4 Sprinkle with parsley and serve.

Ingredients

25g (1oz) butter
1 carrot, diced
1 onion, finely chopped
1 small leek, finely sliced
1 stick celery, finely chopped
1 clove garlic, finely chopped
500ml (1pt) boiling chicken stock
25g (1oz) macaroni
15g (½oz) long grain rice
salt and pepper
200g (8oz) tomatoes, skinned and chopped
2 15ml (tbsp) baked beans
1 5ml (tsp) chopped parsley

Power Level

Full (100%)

Serves 3–4

French Onion

Method

1 Heat the butter in a large shallow dish for 2 (2½) minutes. Toss the onion in the butter then cook for 5 (7) minutes.
2 Add the stock and seasoning and cook for 25 (30) minutes.
3 Cut the toast into small squares and place, buttered side up, on top of the soup. Sprinkle the cheese over and brown under a grill or, melt in the microwave for 2–3 (3–4) minutes.

Note

If the soup is to be frozen the bread and cheese should be omitted until ready for serving.

Ingredients

50g (2oz) butter
400g (1lb) onions, thinly sliced
1l (1¾pt) boiling stock
salt and pepper
2 slices toast, buttered
75g (3oz) cheese, grated

Power Level

Full (100%)

Serves 4–6

Cream of Potato and Onion

Method

1 Peel and dice the potatoes, chop the onions and place both in a large dish. Add the stock and cook for 10–12 (14–16) minutes.
2 Liquidise the soup, returning it to the bowl. Add the milk, seasoning and bouquet garni.
3 Cook for 5 (6) minutes then strain. Adjust seasoning to taste and stir in the cream before serving.

Note

If the soup is to be frozen the cream should be omitted until reheating, ready for serving.

Ingredients

400g (1lb) potatoes
200g (8oz) onion
500ml (1pt) boiling stock
250ml (½pt) milk
salt and pepper
bouquet garni
1 15ml (tbsp) single cream

Power Level

Full (100%)

✻ ✱ ✱ ✱

Serves 4–6

Mulligatawny

Method

Melt the butter in a large bowl for 1 (1½) minutes. Add the onion, carrot, celery and pepper and cook for 3 (5) minutes. Add tomatoes and apple and cook for a further 2 (3) minutes.

Add the stock, curry powder, cloves, parsley, sugar and seasoning. Cook for 10 (12) minutes.

Blend the cornflour with a little milk then stir in the rest of the milk. Stir the milk mixture into the soup then add the meat and rice.

Cook the soup for 5 (7) minutes or until the rice is cooked. Adjust the seasoning and serve.

Ingredients

25g (1oz) butter
1 onion, chopped
1 carrot, diced
2 sticks celery, chopped
½ green pepper, diced
200g (8oz) tomatoes, skinned and chopped
1 apple, peeled and chopped
750ml (1½pt) boiling stock
1 15ml (tbsp) curry powder
2 cloves
1 15ml (tbsp) chopped parsley
1 15ml (tbsp) sugar
salt and pepper
2 15ml (tbsp) cornflour
125ml (¼pt) milk
75–100g (3–4oz) cooked lamb, beef or chicken, finely chopped
25g (1oz) long grain rice

Power Level

Full (100%)

Serves 4–6

Celery

Method

1 Cook the onion in a large bowl for 2 (3) minutes. Wash and chop the celery then add to the onion and cook for 3 (5) minutes.
2 Add the boiling stock, seasoning and herbs. Cook for 10 (12) minutes.
3 Remove bay leaf and bouquet garni. Stir in the dried milk. Liquidise the soup, correct the seasoning and add a few drops of green colouring.
4 Reheat the soup for 4–5 (5–6) minutes and sprinkle with parsley before serving.

Ingredients

1 onion, chopped
½ head of celery (about 5–6 sticks)
750ml (1½pt) white stock, boiling
salt and pepper
bay leaf
bouquet garni
75g (3oz) dried milk
green food colouring
chopped parsley

Power Level

Full (100%)

Serves 4–6

Mussel Chowder

Method

1 Cook the bacon in a large bowl for 2 (3) minutes. Add the onion, celery and pepper and cook for 3 (4) minutes.
2 Add the potato, boiling water, seasoning and bay leaf. Cook for 6 (8) minutes then remove the bay leaf.
3 Blend the flour with a little of the milk then add the remaining milk. Whisk this milk mixture into the soup.
4 Bring the liquid to the boil in the microwave, whisking every 2 minutes (approximately 10 minutes).
5 Add the mussels to the soup and cook for a further 3 (4) minutes. Sprinkle with chopped parsley before serving.

Ingredients

100g (4oz) green streaky bacon, diced
1 onion, chopped
1 stick celery, chopped
1 small green pepper, chopped
2 small potatoes, diced
375ml (¾pt) boiling water
salt and pepper
1 bay leaf
40g (1½oz) plain flour
500ml (1pt) milk
1 283g (10oz) can mussels, drained

Power Level

Full (100%)

Serves 4–6

Sauces

At first glance you may think that it is hardly worth cooking sauces in the microwave as the time saving is very little. However, providing sauces are stirred at intervals during the heating stage, the result is a very smooth sauce and the advantage is that other ingredients can be added for heating or cooking during or after the sauce has cooked, and of course there will be only one dish or bowl to wash.

When making gravy, pour off the meat juices into a gravy boat whilst the joint is in it's final standing period. Add the normal thickening or flavourings and stock. Heat until cooked stirring every minute.

Savoury White Sauce

Method

1 Melt the butter in a medium-sized glass bowl for 1–1½ (1½–2) minutes. Blend in the flour and gradually stir in the milk.
2 Add seasoning and cook for 4–5 (6–7) minutes, stirring every minute. Use as required.

Variations

One of the following ingredients may be added to the sauce 2 minutes before the end of the cooking time:

Prawn sauce: 100g (4oz) peeled prawns
Cheese sauce: 50–75g (2–3oz) cheese, grated
Mushroom sauce: 50g (2oz) mushrooms, chopped
Onion sauce: 100g (4oz) cooked onion, chopped
Parsley sauce: 2 5ml (tsp) parsley, chopped
Egg sauce: 1 hard-boiled egg, chopped finely

Ingredients

25g (1oz) butter
25g (1oz) plain flour
250ml (½pt) milk
salt and pepper

Power Level

Full (100%)

✻ ✱ ✱ ✱

Makes 250ml (½pt)

White Wine Sauce

Method

1 Melt the butter in a small mixing bowl for 1–1½ (1½–2) minutes, stir in the flour and mix well.
2 Cook for 1 (1½) minutes.
3 Pour the wine into a measuring jug and make up to 250ml (¼pt) with milk.
4 Gradually beat the liquids into the butter and flour to give a smooth sauce. Season.
5 Cook for 3–4 (4–5) minutes until boiling and thickened. Stir every minute for the first two minutes and every 30 seconds after that.

The variations for white sauce may also be used for the wine sauce.

Ingredients

25g (1oz) butter
25g (1oz) plain flour
salt and pepper
1 wineglass white wine
milk

Power Level

Full (100%)

Makes 250ml (½pt)

Tomato Sauce

Method

1 Melt the butter for 1 (1½) minutes. Add the onion and bacon and cook covered, for 3 (4) minutes.
2 Add the other ingredients and cook for 5 (7) minutes, stirring once.
3 Sieve and adjust seasoning to taste.

Ingredients

15g (½oz) butter
½ onion, chopped
2 rashers bacon, chopped
15g (½oz) plain flour
1 397g (14oz) can tomatoes
1 clove
1 bay leaf
few sprigs of rosemary
salt and pepper

Power Level
Full (100%)

![*][***]

Makes about 250ml (½pt)

Barbecue Sauce

Method

1 Melt the butter, in the microwave, for 1 (1½) minutes. Add the onion and cook for 3 (4) minutes.
2 Add the remaining ingredients, stir well and cook for 3 (5) minutes.

Note

Serve the sauce with beefburgers, chicken or any barbecued food.

Ingredients

15g (½oz) butter
1 onion, finely chopped
2 5ml (tsp) Worcestershire sauce
6 15ml (tbsp) tomato ketchup
200ml (8fl oz) water
salt and pepper

Power Level
Full (100%)

![*][***]

Makes about 250ml (½pt)

Bread Sauce

Method

1 Peel the onion but leave it whole. Place in a bowl with the cloves, milk and salt. Heat for 3 (4) minutes.
2 Add the other ingredients and cook for 5 (6) minutes, stirring once during cooking.
3 Remove the onion, cloves, peppercorns and bay leaf, then beat well. Beat in an extra 15g (½oz) butter if required.

Ingredients

1 medium-sized onion
2 cloves
375ml (¾pt) milk
pinch of salt
6 peppercorns
1 bay leaf
25g (1oz) butter
75g (3oz) breadcrumbs

Power Level
Full (100%)

![*][***]

Makes 375ml (¾pt)

Hollandaise Sauce

Method

1 Melt the butter on 50% setting for 2 (4) minutes. Add the other ingredients and whisk lightly.
2 Cook on 50% setting for 1 (2) minutes, then whisk well, season and serve immediately.

Note

The sauce may be served with fish, e.g. salmon steaks or broccoli or asparagus spears as a starter to a meal

Ingredients

100g (4oz) butter
2 15ml (tbsp) wine vinegar
2 egg yolks
salt and pepper

Power Level

50%

Makes about 125ml (¼pt)

Custard

Method

1 Mix the sugar and custard powder with a little of the milk. Gradually add the rest of the milk.
2 Cook for 2 minutes, stir. Repeat this operation until thick. (approximately 8 (10) minutes).

Ingredients

2 15ml (tbsp) sugar
2 15ml (tbsp) custard powder
500ml (1pt) milk

Power Level

Full (100%)

Makes 500ml (1pt)

Traditional Custard Sauce

Method

1 Place the egg yolks in a bowl with the sugar and mix well.
2 Blend the cornflour smoothly with the milk and heat in the cooker for 2–3 (3–4) minutes, stirring every minute.
3 Pour the milk onto the egg and sugar mixture and stir well. Add the vanilla essence and stir again. Cook for 2 (3) minutes, stirring every 30 seconds.

Note

The custard can be cooked for 4–4½ (5–5½) minutes on 50% setting to avoid overcooking.

Ingredients

2 egg yolks
25g (1oz) caster sugar
15g (½oz) cornflour
250ml (½pt) milk
few drops of vanilla essence

Power Level

Full (100%) or 50%

Makes 250ml (½pt)

Apple Sauce

Method

- Peel and core the apples and slice thinly. Cook with the other ingredients in a covered dish or roasting bag for 6–8 (10–12) minutes.
- When cooked, remove lemon peel, beat well or sieve. Reheat and use as required.

Ingredients

400g (1lb) cooking apples
15g (½oz) butter
sugar to taste
1 strip lemon peel
1 15ml (tbsp) water

Power Level

Full (100%)

Makes 250ml (½pt)

Chocolate Sauce

Method

- Place the chocolate and the water in a bowl and melt for 1 (1½) minutes. Stir well.
- Add the evaporated milk, cornflour, and sugar. Cook for 1 (1½) minutes, stirring every 30 seconds.
- Allow to cool slightly then add the vanilla essence. Beat well. Serve hot or cold.

Ingredients

50g (2oz) plain chocolate
2 15ml (tbsp) water
1 5ml (tsp) cornflour
1 5ml (tsp) caster sugar
50ml (2fl oz) evaporated milk
½ 5ml (tsp) vanilla essence

Power Level

Full (100%)

Makes 125ml (¼pt)

Jam Sauce

Method

Place the jam and 250ml (½pt) water in a bowl and heat in the cooker for 4–6 (5–7) minutes. Blend the arrowroot with the cold water and add to the jam.
Add the lemon juice and cook for 2–3 (3–4) minutes, stirring every minute.

Ingredients

200g (8oz) jam
250ml (½pt) water or fruit juice
4 5ml (tsp) arrowroot
4 15ml (tbsp) cold water
squeeze of lemon juice

Power Level

Full (100%)

Makes about 375ml (¾pt)

Butterscotch Sauce

Method

1 Heat the sugar in a bowl for 30 (45) seconds. Add the butter and syrup.
2 Heat on 50% setting for 1 (2) minutes then stir thoroughly adding almonds and lemon juice if desired.
3 Heat on 50% setting for 3–4 (5–6) minutes, stirring every minute, or until sugar dissolves.

Note

Use the sauce as a topping for ice-cream and desserts.

Ingredients

50g (2oz) light, soft brown sugar
50g (2oz) butter
2 15ml (tbsp) golden syrup
15g (½oz) flaked almonds, chopped*
squeeze of lemon juice*
(* optional)

Power Level

50%

Makes about 125ml (¼pt)

Cranberry Sauce

Method

1 Wash, top and tail the cranberries. Place the fruit in a covered dish or roasting bag and add the sugar and water.
2 Cook in the microwave for 5–6 (7–8) minutes, or until fruit is soft.

Note

Serve the sauce with roast turkey or chicken.

Ingredients

400g (1lb) cranberries
100g (4oz) sugar
1 15ml (tbsp) water

Power Level

Full (100%)

Makes about 375ml (¾pt)

Yeast

The advantage of proving dough in the microwave is that it is so fast – a ½kg (1lb) of white or brown dough can be proved in 20–30 minutes. The covered dough is given small amounts of microwave energy (about 15 seconds) and then left to heat equalize for 5–10 minutes. This ensures an even growth of the yeast and after repeating the energy and rest periods the dough will double in size rapidly. After proving and shaping the dough it can be cooked in the microwave in 6–7 (7–8) minutes. This will produce a good textured loaf with a soft crust. Of course it will not be browned as when baking conventionally but if a crisper crust is preferred, the dough can be partly cooked for 3–4 (4–5) minutes in the microwave oven and then finished off in a conventional oven preheated to a high temperature, for 8–10 minutes.

Loaves of bread or rolls which are to be completely cooked by microwave can be sprinkled with nibbed wheat or poppy seeds for a more decorative finish.

Pizza

Method

Heat the oil in a large bowl for 3 (4) minutes. Add the onion and garlic and cook for 3 (4) minutes.

Add tomatoes and seasonings and cook until fairly thick, about 2 (3) minutes.

Divide the dough into 4 pieces. Roll out each piece to a circle and use to cover 4 20cm (8in) plates. Prove each one for 15 seconds leave for 5 minutes then repeat this once or twice until doubled in size.

Divide the topping between the pizza bases. Spread over the bases then sprinkle with grated cheese and decorate with anchovies and olives.

Cook the pizzas, one at a time, for 4 (5½) minutes, turning every minute.

Variations

Either 50–75g (2–3oz) sardines, cooked bacon, mushrooms or prawns can be added to the sauce with the tomatoes.

Ingredients

400g (1lb) basic white bread dough (see page 62)

For the sauce
2 15ml (tbsp) oil
2 medium-sized onions, chopped
1 clove garlic, finely chopped
1 425g (15oz) can tomatoes
1 5ml (tsp) oregano
salt and pepper
200g (8oz) Cheddar cheese, grated
anchovy fillets and olives to decorate

Power Level

Full (100%)

✳✳✳✳

Makes 4 pizzas

White Bread

Method

1 Mix the sugar with 75ml (3fl oz) of the water and warm in the microwave for 15–30 (30–45) seconds. Sprinkle on the yeast and leave to activate.
2 Place the flour and salt in a bowl and rub in the fat. Add the yeast liquid and the rest of the water and knead well. Add a little extra water if necessary.
3 Prove the bread dough in a bowl covered with cling wrap for 15 seconds then leave to stand for 10 minutes. Repeat this 3–4 times until the dough has doubled in size.
4 Knock back lightly and continue as follows for a white loaf, or use as required for pizzas or rolls.
5 Shape the dough and place in a greased dish with the bottom lined with greased greaseproof paper. A 15cm (6in) plain souffle dish is ideal.
6 Warm in the microwave for 15 seconds, stand for 5 minutes. Repeat this 1 or 2 times or until the dough is well risen.
7 Cook for 5 (6) minutes, turn, cook for 2 (3) minutes. Leave for 10 minutes then turn out onto a wire cooling rack.

Ingredients

1 5ml (tsp) sugar
250ml (½pt) water
7g (¼oz) dried yeast
400g (1lb) plain flour
1 5ml (tsp) salt
25g (1oz) butter

Power Level

Full (100%)

✳✳✳✳

Variation

For **Brown Bread** substitute 200g (8oz) wholemeal flour for half th white flour. Make up and cook as above.

Bread Rolls

Method

1 Divide the dough into 16 pieces. Shape into rolls and place on the glass shelf.
2 Heat for 15 seconds, leave for 5 minutes. Repeat this 3 times, or until the rolls have doubled in size.
3 For soft rolls cook in the microwave for 7–8 (8–9) minutes. For crisp rolls bake conventionally for 15 minutes at 220°C (425°F, Gas Mark 7).

Note

For smaller models it may be necessary to cook the rolls 8 at a time for 3–4 (4–5) minutes.

Ingredients

400g (1lb) basic white bread dough (see above)

Power Level

Full (100%)

Makes 16 rolls

Chelsea Bun Ring

Method

Grease a 20cm (8in) round flan dish. Warm the sugar and milk for 15–30 (30–45) seconds. Sprinkle on the yeast and leave to activate.

Place the flour and salt in a large bowl and rub in 25g (1oz) butter. Add the yeast liquid and knead to a soft dough.

Warm in the microwave in a bowl covered with cling wrap for 15 seconds then leave for 5 minutes. Repeat this 3–4 times, or until the dough has doubled in size.

Knock the dough back and roll out to a 25–30cm (10–12in) square. Melt the remaining 25g (1oz) butter for 30 (60) seconds and brush over the dough.

Sprinkle the currants and sugar over the square. Damp the edges and roll up the dough to give a long 'sausage'. Cut this into 8 slices.

Place the slices in the dish, cut side down and cover loosely with cling wrap.

Ingredients

1 5ml (tsp) sugar
125ml (¼pt) milk
7g (¼oz) dried yeast
200g (8oz) plain flour
½ 5ml (tsp) salt
50g (2oz) butter
100g (4oz) currants
25–50g (1–2oz) caster sugar
apricot glaze (see page 64)
glacé icing

Power Level
Full (100%)

✳✳✳✳

7 Heat for 30 seconds, leave for 5 minutes. Repeat this 2–3 times until doubled in size. Remove the cling wrap and cook for 5 (7) minutes.

8 Turn the bun ring out of the dish and brush with apricot glaze. Drizzle glacé icing over the top of the ring before serving.

Malt Loaf

Method

Lightly grease a small round dish. In a separate small bowl warm the sugar and water for 15–30 (30–45) seconds, sprinkle on the yeast and leave to activate.

Sieve the flour and salt and add the sultanas. Warm the malt, treacle and butter for 15–30 (30–45) seconds.

Add the yeast liquid and syrup to the flour, mixing to a soft, sticky dough adding more water if necessary.

Knead until smooth. Shape and place in the prepared dish.

Warm in the microwave for 15 seconds, leave for 5 minutes, give dish ¼ turn. Repeat until dough has doubled in size.

Cook for 4–5 (6–7) minutes, turning once during cooking time. Cool slightly before turning out onto a wire cooling rack. Brush with apricot glaze and served sliced with butter.

Ingredients

1 5ml (tsp) sugar
125ml (¼pt) water
7g (¼oz) dried yeast
200g (8oz) plain flour
½ 5ml (tsp) salt
50g (2oz) sultanas
2 15ml (tbsp) malt extract
2 5ml (tsp) black treacle
15g (½oz) butter
apricot glaze (see page 64)

Power Level
Full (100%)

✳✳✳✳

Makes 1 loaf

Savarin

Method

1 Warm the water and sugar for 15–30 (30–45) seconds. Sprinkle on the yeast and leave to activate.

2 Add the yeast liquid to the flour and salt. Mix and knead well. The dough should be fairly soft, add a little more liquid if necessary.

3 Return the dough to the bowl, cover with cling wrap. Warm for 15 seconds, leave for 5 minutes. Repeat 3–4 times, or until dough has doubled in size.

4 Grease a 22.5cm (9in) microwave savarin mould and arrange a few halved, blanched almonds in the bottom.

5 Melt the butter for 1½–2 (2–2½) minutes. Beat the eggs and butter into the dough gradually, until the mixture becomes a rich batter. Beat well.

6 Carefully spoon or pour the batter into the mould. Cover with cling wrap. Warm in the microwave for 15–30 seconds, give ¼ turn, leave to stand for 5 minutes. Repeat this until the mixture reaches the top of the mould.

7 Cook for 10 (12) minutes. Cool for 2–3 minutes then turn onto a wire cooling rack.

8 Make the syrup by heating the sugar and water in a small bowl for 8 (9½) minutes, or until a thick syrup forms. Stir in the flavourings and pour over the savarin.

9 Allow the savarin to cool completely. Place on a large serving dish and brush with the apricot glaze. Make the glaze by mixing the jam with the hot water.

10 Fill the centre of the savarin with fresh or canned fruit salad. Pipe with whipped cream. Extra fruit can be arranged around the base of the savarin if desired.

Note

The basic savarin ring is suitable for freezing.

Ingredients

125ml (¼pt) water
1 5ml (tsp) sugar
15g (½oz) dried yeast
225g (9oz) plain flour
½ 5ml (tsp) salt
50g (2oz) butter
2 eggs, beaten
few blanched almonds

For the syrup

100g (4oz) caster sugar
125ml (¼pt) water
few drops of lemon juice
few drops of rum or other flavouring

For the apricot glaze

4 15ml (tbsp) apricot jam, sieved
2–3 15ml (tbsp) hot water

Power Level

Full (100%)

✳❋❋❋

Fish

Fresh or frozen fish cooked in the microwave is simply out of this world, full of flavour and cooked to perfection. Whether 'steaming' 'baking' or 'poaching' fresh or frozen fish, whole or filleted, it should be covered during cooking in the microwave. Normally a little melted butter and/or lemon juice is sufficient additional moisture. Sprinkle with seasoning, paprika or herbs to enhance the appearance and flavour. Thin ends of the fish may be covered with aluminium foil when defrosting or cooking to prevent overcooking of these thinner parts. Test the fish at regular intervals during cooking. When it is cooked it will flake. Breadcrumbed fish can be dotted with butter and cooked although the breadcrumb coating will not become crisp unless using a browning dish. Do not deep fat fry in the microwave as the temperature of the fat cannot be controlled. Boil in the bag fish should have bag slit before cooking.

Before defrosting frozen fish, please read section 'Use of the Defrost Control or Setting' for those microwave models with defrost control or setting.

Fish Defrosting and Cooking Chart

Fish	Weight	Defrost Instructions on Full (100%)	Defrost Instructions on 50% Setting	Cooking Times
White fish, e.g. cod, haddock, coley fillets or cutlets, whole plaice or sole	400g (1 lb) prepared fillets or fish gutted	Cook for 4–5 (5–6) minutes Stand for 5 minutes	Cook for 5 (7) minutes Stand for 5 minutes Cook for 3 (4) minutes Stand for 5 minutes	6–8 (8–10) minutes
Smoked fish, e.g. smoked haddock, cod	400g (1 lb) prepared fillets	Cook for 5 (6) minutes Stand for 5 minutes	Cook for 5 (7) minutes Stand for 5 minutes Cook for 3 (4) minutes Stand for 3 minutes	4–5 (6–8) minutes
Mackerel	2 250–300g (10–12oz) fish, gutted but whole	Cook for 3 (4) minutes Turn Cook for 2 (3) minutes Stand for 5 minutes (Bone when thawed)	Cook for 5 (7) minutes Stand for 5 minutes Cook for 2–3 (3–4) minutes Stand for 3 minutes (Bone when thawed)	8–10 (10–12) minutes
Kippers	400g (1lb) prepared fillets	Cook for 3–4 (4–6) minutes Stand for 5 minutes	Cook for 4–6 (5–7) minutes Stand for 3 minutes	3–4 (5–6) minutes
Herrings and Trout	2 200g (8oz) fish, gutted but whole	Cook for 3 (4) minutes Stand for 3 minutes Cook for 2 (3) minutes Stand for 2 minutes (Bone when thawed)	Cook for 4 (5) minutes Stand for 4 minutes Cook for 4 (5) minutes Stand for 5 minutes (Bone when thawed)	6–8 (8–10) minutes
Shell fish, e.g. scampi, prawns	400g (1 lb) prepared prawns	Cook for 3 (4) minutes Stand for 10 minutes	Cook for 4 (5) minutes Stand for 5 minutes Cook for 3 (4) minutes Stand for 10 minutes	Use as recipe directs

Cod Steaks with Leek and Corn Stuffing

Method

1 Slice the leek and place in a bowl with 2 15ml (tbsp) salted water. Cover with cling film and cook for 3 (4) minutes.

2 Melt the butter, in the microwave, for 1 (1½) minutes. Add to the leek with the breadcrumbs, cheese, seasoning and sweetcorn, reserving 2 15ml (tbsp) of sweetcorn for garnish.

3 Chop one of the tomatoes and add it to the mixture. Bind the stuffing with the beaten egg.

4 Wash and trim the fish. Place in a large casserole and season lightly. Cover and cook for 5 (7) minutes then stand for 5 minutes.

5 Stuff the cavity of each cod steak with the leek mixture and cover the end of each steak with mixture as well.

6 Slice the remaining tomato and place one slice on each steak. Sprinkle on the reserved corn.

7 Cover and cook for 3 (4) minutes, turn and cook for 3 (4) minutes. Serve immediately.

Ingredients

1 leek, washed and trimmed
40g (1½oz) butter
50g (2oz) white breadcrumbs
40g (1½oz) Cheddar cheese, grated
1 326g (11½oz) can sweetcorn
salt and pepper
2 tomatoes, skinned
1 egg, beaten
4 cod steaks, weighing about 150g (6oz) each

Power Level

Full (100%)

Serves 4

Scampi Provençale

Method

1 Melt the butter in a casserole dish for 2 (2½) minutes. Toss the onion and garlic in the butter and cook for 4 (5) minutes.

2 Add tomatoes, wine, seasoning, sugar and parsley. Stir well and heat for 3 (4) minutes.

3 Drain the scampi well, add to the sauce and continue simmering for about 2 (3) minutes or until just heated through. Serve with freshly boiled rice.

Ingredients

25g (1oz) butter
1 onion, chopped
1 clove garlic, chopped
1 397g (14oz) can tomatoes, drained
5 15ml (tbsp) dry white wine
salt and pepper
pinch of sugar
1 15ml (tbsp) chopped parsley
200g (8oz) frozen scampi, thawed
boiled rice (see 'Vegetables')

Power Level

Full (100%)

Serves 4

Sole Veronique

Method

1 Trim the fillets, wash, wipe and lay them in a large, shallow dish. Add the onion, mushrooms, herbs, seasoning, wine and water. Cook for 5 (7) minutes
2 Place the grapes in hot water for a few minutes, then peel, halve and remove pips, reserving a few halves for decoration.
3 Melt the butter in a large bowl, for 1 (1½) minutes, stir in the flour and the fish stock, made up to 250ml (½pt) with the milk. Cook in the microwave for 3–4 (4–5) minutes, stirring every minute.
4 Stir in the grapes, lemon juice and cream and pour the sauce over the fish. Reheat in the microwave for 3 (4) minutes then decorate with the reserved grapes and serve.

Ingredients

2 soles, filleted
3 slices onion
50g (2oz) button mushrooms, sliced
few sprigs of parsley
1 bay leaf
salt and pepper
125ml (¼pt) dry white wine
125ml (¼pt) water
100g (4oz) white grapes
25g (1oz) butter
25g (1oz) plain flour
125ml (¼pt) milk
squeeze of lemon juice
2 15ml (tbsp) single cream

Power Level
Full (100%)

Serves 4

Trout and Almonds

Method

1 Clean the fish, leaving the heads on. Wash and dry. Place in the serving dish, season lightly and add a few drops of lemon juice.
2 Melt the butter, in the microwave, for 2 (2½) minutes. Brush the trout with the butter, cover with kitchen paper and cook for 6 (8) minutes.
3 Sprinkle almonds over the fish and cook for a further 2–4 (5–6) minutes, depending on the size of the fish. Larger fish will take 1–2 minutes longer.

Ingredients

4 trout (about 100–125g (4–5oz) each)
salt and pepper
few drops of lemon juice
50g (2oz) butter
50–75g (2–3oz) blanched almonds, cut into slivers

Power Level
Full (100%)

Serves 4

Skate with Caper Butter

Method

1 Cut each wing into 3 wedges. Place in a large, shallow dish covered in cling wrap and cook for 5 (7) minutes.
2 Melt and cook the butter for 5 (6) minutes. Add the capers, vinegar, parsley and seasoning and cook for 2 (3) minutes.
3 Skin the skate and lay the pieces in the serving dish. Pour the butter over the fish, cover and reheat for 3–4 (4–5) minutes.

Ingredients

2 wings of skate (about 400g (1lb) each)
50–75g (2–3oz) butter
1 15ml (tbsp) capers
5 15ml (tbsp) wine vinegar
1 15ml (tbsp) chopped parsley
salt and pepper

Power Level
Full (100%)

Serves 3–4

Kedgeree

Method

1 Place the boiling water in a large casserole dish. Add the salt and stir in the rice. Cover and cook for 15 (18) minutes. Leave to stand for 10 minutes, when all the water should be absorbed but if not, drain the rice.

2 Wash and trim the fish, place in an ovenware dish and cover with cling wrap. Cook for 4 (6) minutes. Flake the fish, discarding the skin and bones.

3 Chop one hard-boiled egg and slice the other. Melt the butter in a large dish for 2 (2½) minutes. Toss the onion in the butter. Cook for 4 (5) minutes.

4 Add the rice, fish, chopped hard-boiled egg and seasoning. Mix well and warm through for 3–4 (4–5) minutes.

5 Garnish with sliced hard-boiled egg and chopped parsley before serving.

Note

Kedgeree is traditionally a breakfast dish but also makes a substantial supper dish.

Ingredients

450ml (18fl oz) boiling water
pinch of salt
150g (6oz) long grain rice
300g (12oz) smoked haddock
2 hard-boiled eggs
50g (2oz) butter
1 small onion, chopped
salt and pepper
1 15ml (tbsp) chopped parsley

Power Level

Full (100%)

✳✳✳✳

Serves 6–8

Roll Mops

Method

1 Clean and bone the herrings. Roll up tightly from the tail end. Secure with a wooden cocktail stick if necessary.

2 Place in a shallow dish with the herbs, seasoning and onion. Mix the water and vinegar together and pour over the fish. Cover the dish with a lid or cling wrap with a slit in the middle.

3 Cook in the microwave for 6 (8) minutes. Allow to cool in the cooking liquor.

Ingredients

4 fresh herrings
1 blade mace
1 bay leaf
2 cloves
6 peppercorns
pinch of salt
1 onion, chopped
125ml (¼pt) water
125ml (¼pt) vinegar

Power Level

Full (100%)

✳✳✳✳

Serves 4

Mackerel with Watercress Sauce

Method

1 Place the watercress in a large bowl with the salt and boiling water and cook for 4 (5) minutes. Drain.
2 Liquidise the watercress with the anchovy fillets, 40g (1½oz) butter, salt and peppers.
3 Melt 7g (¼oz) butter for 15 (30) seconds, add the flour, purée and stock. Cook for 3 (5) minutes, stirring once during cooking.
4 Wash and dry the mackerel fillets and lay them in the serving dish. Season and sprinkle with lemon juice. Pour the sauce over the fish and cook for 5–6 (7–8) minutes, turning the dish once during cooking. Decorate with twists of lemon before serving.

Ingredients

2 bunches watercress, washed and trimmed
pinch of salt
500ml (1pt) boiling water
2 anchovy fillets
40g (1½oz) butter
salt and pepper
cayenne pepper
7g (¼oz) butter
7g (¼oz) plain flour
250ml (½pt) white stock
400g (1lb) mackerel fillets
few drops of lemon juice
lemon twists

Power Level
Full (100%)

Serves 4

Mixed Fish Curry

Method

1 Mix the basil, spices, garlic and cornflour to a paste with a little water.
2 Melt the butter in a large bowl for 1 (1½) minutes, add the onion and cook for 3 (4) minutes.
3 Add the paste gradually then add all the other ingredients except the fish.
4 Cook for 3–4 (5–6) minutes, stirring every minute, until thickened. Add the fish and heat through for 2 (3) minutes. Serve with freshly boiled rice.

Ingredients

generous pinch of sweet basil
1 5ml (tsp) cumin powder
1 5ml (tsp) chilli powder
½ 5ml (tsp) ground tumeric
1 clove garlic, crushed
2 15ml (tbsp) cornflour
25g (1oz) butter
1 onion, sliced
pinch of salt
2 tomatoes, skinned and chopped
2 5ml (tsp) coconut, softened in a little milk
250ml (½pt) water
pinch of sugar
juice of ½ lemon
1½l (3pt) prawns (about 250g (10ọz) after shelling)
any cooked, white fish to make up to 400g (1lb) with the prawns
boiled rice (see 'Vegetables')

Power Level
Full (100%)

Serves 4

Crab Gratinée Diable

Method

1 Melt the butter, in a bowl, for 1 (1½) minutes. Add the prepared crab meat, cheese, breadcrumbs, cream and seasonings.
2 Mix thoroughly and carefully spoon back into the cleaned crab shell, or, into a small bowl.
3 Cook for 2 (3) minutes, stand for 5 minutes, turn, cook for 2 (3) minutes.
4 Slice the banana thinly and dip in the lemon juice to prevent slices from browning. Place around the outside of the shell or dish and cook for 1 (1½) minutes.
5 Sprinkle with chopped parsley and serve with dry biscuits or fingers of toast.

Ingredients

25g (1oz) butter
1 dressed crab, or 300g (12oz) canned or frozen crabmeat
25g (1oz) cheese, grated
2 15ml (tbsp) fresh white breadcrumbs
1 15ml (tbsp) single cream or top of the milk
pinch of dry mustard
pinch of cayenne pepper
salt and pepper
dash of anchovy essence
1 firm banana
few drops of lemon juice
1 15ml (tbsp) chopped parsley
dry biscuits or fingers of toast

Power Level

Full (100%)

Serves 2–4

Fish Pie

Method

1 Put the soup and milk into an ovenware dish. Heat for 1 (2) minutes, stir, heat for 2 (3) minutes. Mix thoroughly.
2 Add the peas and cooked fish and pour into a 750ml (1½pt) pie dish. Cook for 4 (5) minutes, stirring once during cooking.
3 Sprinkle half the crisps on top of the mixture, cover with the cheese and top with the remaining crisps.
4 Cook for 1½ (2½) minutes, or until the cheese is melted. Sprinkle with chopped parsley and serve.

Note

Crisp topping should be added after thawing.

Ingredients

1 298g (10½oz) can condensed vegetable soup
125ml (¼pt) milk
3 15ml (tbsp) frozen peas
400g (1lb) cooked fish
salt and pepper
75g (3oz) crisps (cheese and onion or plain)
50g (2oz) Cheddar cheese, grated
1 15ml (tbsp) chopped parsley

Power Level

Full (100%)

Serves 4

Meat and Poultry

Whether using joints or smaller cuts, meat can be cooked successfully in the microwave cooker. Whilst the meat is resting during its final heat equalization period, vegetables, sauces, gravy, etc., can be quickly cooked to produce a complete microwave meal.

The advantage of cooking meat casseroles by microwave is that they can be prepared well in advance, refrigerated or even frozen and just reheated when required. We have found that casseroles using cheaper cuts of meat, which have been microwave cooked, left to cool and then reheated appear to benefit from the latent heat and in fact can be more tender than those which are cooked and served immediately.

Defrosting

Although thinner cuts of meat can be thawed and cooked in one heating operation, generally it is better to ensure that all meat and poultry is completely defrosted before cooking to ensure even results. This can be carried out by using the microwave, or by thawing naturally or a combination of both, commencing the defrosting in the microwave and then leaving the meat to thaw thoroughly in the refrigerator, larder or at room temperature.

When defrosting by microwave, thinner ends of joints and smaller cuts can be protected with smooth pieces of aluminium foil which prevent the outer sections from beginning to cook whilst the centre parts are still thawing. If some cooking does begin during defrosting, this is acceptable providing the meat is to be cooked immediately afterwards, although the cooked parts should be protected with aluminium foil during the cooking process.

To ensure even defrosting, the food should be turned halfway through defrosting and smaller cuts such as chops, steak, chicken portions and sausages should be separated and turned as soon as possible after defrosting begins. When defrosting sausage meat or minced meat, the thawed portions can be removed leaving the still frozen part to be returned to the microwave.

Most meats require standing time to allow heat equalisation during defrosting so that the outer parts will not begin to cook whilst the centre is still frozen, but we have found that foods covered with clingwrap or placed in a roasting bag will retain more moisture and that defrosting will be slightly faster.

Meat thermometers must not be used in the microwave during a heating cycle. Only specially designed thermometers may be left inside the oven whilst it is operating. The use of a thermometer is helpful to determine the centre temperature of food, particularly when thawing larger cuts and joints.

For those models with a defrost control or setting, please read the section 'Use of the Defrost Control or Setting' on page 14.

Cooking

A joint will have a better appearance and cook more evenly if it is a regular shape. Ideal cuts are top leg of pork, lamb and rolled joints. If the meat is not uniform in size, the narrower sections may be covered with a smooth piece of aluminium foil for half the cooking time. Poultry should have the wings and legs tied closely to the body and any projecting parts should be protected by covering them with foil.

Seasonings may be sprinkled over the meat but salt attracts moisture and may cause a hardening effect of the outer edges during cooking. If in doubt, leave seasoning until after cooking. The exception to this is the skin on pork which should be scored with a knife and rubbed with salt to help obtain a crisp crackling.

Roasting bags are ideal for cooking all joints in the microwave, but do remember not to use the paper/metal ties; string or rubber bands are suitable and may be used instead. Alternatively, meat may be cooked in a covered casserole dish or can be 'open' roasted. This latter method is preferable when cooking pork with crackling as it allows a certain amount of moisture to 'escape'. When 'open' roasting the joint is placed on an inverted small flat dish or a plate which is used as a trivet inside the roasting dish. Specially designed microwave roasting dishes and trivets are now available on the market. These keep the joint out of its own juices during cooking but the meat should be lightly covered with greaseproof paper or kitchen paper to prevent splatterings on to the oven interior. It is preferable to turn larger joints at least once during their cooking period and they should be allowed to stand for 10–25 minutes halfway through. Joints which have fat on one side only should be placed with the fat side down at commencement of cooking and turned fat side up halfway through the cooking period.

If the total cooking time is 15 minutes or more the joint will brown naturally but for extra browning the joint may be placed in a conventional oven at a high temperature for 10–15 minutes at the end of the cooking period. The careful use of gravy brownings, sauces or paprika pepper, painted or sprinkled on to the surface of the joint will give a more attractive colour if required.

At the end of the microwave cooking period allow the joint to stand for at least 5 minutes and up to 20 minutes to heat equalise. The joint will carry on cooking slightly during this period but either leave it in the roasting bag or cover it with aluminium foil to retain the heat. However, if it is cooked to the desired degree on completion of the cooking time, it is not necessary to let it stand.

Casseroles

Casseroles and stews can be prepared and cooked in the microwave cooker on 50% for the total cooking time or on full (100%) for half the cooking time and then reduce to 50% for the remaining time. This will allow food flavourings and seasonings to blend during this slower cooking stage. Casseroles may be frozen as a whole or in individual portions and reheated either on full (100%), stirring from time to time and allowing approximately 1 minute per 25g (1oz) or on 50% for a longer, slower period.

Points to remember:

1 The tenderness of meat casseroles is improved if the dish is left to cool after microwave cooking and then reheated when required.
2 A joint will have a better appearance and cook more evenly if it is a regular shape.
3 Smooth pieces of aluminium foil may be used to protect the thinner or narrower ends of meat during defrosting and/or cooking.
4 Meat and poultry should be fully thawed before cooking.
5 Joints should be turned halfway through the cooking cycle.
6 Standing time is required by most joints at the end of the cooking time but larger joints require a standing time halfway through their cooking period.
7 Allow an extra minute per pound when cooking stuffed poultry.

The defrosting and cooking charts are based on meats which have been removed straight from the freezer for defrosting and are fully thawed before cooking. If meats are partially thawed before defrosting or are not completely thawed before cooking then the times on these charts will require some adjustment to suit. For those models with a defrost control or setting do not forget to read the section on page 14.

Given below are the defrosting and cooking times per $^1/_2$kg (1lb) to enable you to take any joint from your freezer, defrost it and then cook it in your microwave cooker.

The defrosting and cooking times on this chart include timings for both lower and higher output cookers. Models with a lower output will require the longer times and those with a higher output will require the shorter times (i.e. Beef medium rare is cooked for 5–7 minutes).

POINTS TO REMEMBER

1. Resting time allows the heat to equalise throughout the food during defrosting, and is required whether the defrost control is used or not. When following our defrosting times per $^1/_2$kg (1lb) remember to allow resting times during the defrosting period.

2. Although better defrosting results are achieved using 50% power, if time is limited defrosting on full (100%) may be preferred.

Meat	M/W Defrost Time $^1/_2$ kg (1lb)		M/W Cook Time $^1/_2$kg (1lb)	Cook Resting Time
	Full (100%)	or 50%		
Beef *Rolled, boned*	5–7 mins +resting time	8–10 mins +resting time	Rare=4–6 mins Med=5–7 mins Well=6–8 mins	
Beef *Joints on bone*	7–8 mins +resting time	12 mins +resting time	Rare=4–6 mins Med=5–7 mins Well=6–8 mins	
Lamb or Veal *Leg*	4–5 mins +resting time	6 mins +resting time	7–9 mins	
Lamb or Veal *Shoulder*	3–4 mins +resting time	5 mins +resting time	7–9 mins	Joints should be rested half way through the cooking period and at least 5 minutes at the end of cooking. (See notes on page 73.)
Pork *Top leg of pork*	3–4 mins +resting time	7–8 mins +resting time	7–9 mins	
Poultry Chicken *Whole unboned*	4–5 mins +resting time	6–7 mins +resting time	5–7 mins	
Turkey *Whole unboned*		18 mins +resting time	6–8 mins	
Duckling *Whole unboned*	4–5 mins +resting time	6–7 mins +resting time	5–7 mins	

To help you to plan the best way of defrosting and cooking your joint we have then taken an example of each type of meat and poultry, given its weight and then the total defrosting and cooking times for each example.

The resting approximate times required during the defrosting period for each example are also given in the chart below.

These are total resting times required and a better result is obtained if this time is spread evenly throughout the defrosting period, allowing short bursts of microwave energy interspersed with resting times.

Longer periods of microwave energy with resting times will obtain a quicker defrost, but may result in less even thawing.

EXAMPLE

Joints and Weights	Total M/W Defrosting Time 'Full' (100%)	50%	-PLUS-Total Approximate Defrosting Resting Time	Total M/W Cook Time (After Defrosting)	Plus Cook Resting Time (see p. 74)	Any other points
topside, $1\frac{1}{2}$ kg (3lb)	18 mins	27 mins	45–60 mins	18 mins		Turn joint on sides during defrosting.
rib, 2kg (4lb)	30 mins	48 mins	50–70 mins	24 mins		Cover bone end with foil during defrosting.
$1\frac{3}{4}$kg ($3\frac{1}{2}$lb) joint	15 mins	21 mins	30–40 mins	28 mins		Cover knuckle end of lamb with foil once thawed.
$1\frac{1}{2}$kg (3lb) joint	11 mins	15 mins	30–50 mins	24 mins	Generally 10–25 minutes half way through cooking and at least 5 minutes at the end.	Foreleg and rib (if any) may need covering with foil during defrosting.
2kg (4lb) joint	14 mins	30 mins	50–70 mins	32 mins		Try to get an evenly shaped joint. Tie for roasting after thawing.
$1\frac{1}{2}$kg (3lb)	12–15 mins	23 mins	15–30 mins	18 mins		Drumsticks may need to be covered with foil for the first half of the cooking period, to prevent overcooking.
5kg ($10\frac{1}{4}$lb)		180 mins	200–210 mins	72 mins		
$1\frac{3}{4}$kg ($3\frac{1}{2}$lb)	15 mins	23 mins	30–40 mins	21 mins		Legs may need to be covered with foil as for chicken.

Type or Cut of Meat	Weight	Defrosting Time 'Full' (100%)	50%	Standing Time 'Full' (100%)	50%	Special Points	Cooking
Stewing or braising meat, e.g. beef or lamb	600g (1½lb)	6 (7) mins	11 (12) mins	10 mins	10 mins	Separate pieces of meat during defrosting.	Use as required
Minced beef	400g (1lb)	7 (8) mins	10 (11) mins	11 mins	11 mins	Break up during defrosting. Remove thawed meat from oven.	Use as required or add seasoning and 3 15ml (tbsp) water or stock and cook for 5 (7) mins
Belly pork strips	400g (1lb) (4 strips)	2 (3) mins	4 (5) mins	4 mins	5 mins	Separate strips during defrosting.	Use as required or cook for 8–10 (10–12) mins turning during cooking
Offal (liver and kidney)	400g (1lb)	5 (6) mins	9 (10) mins	4 mins	4 mins	Separate pieces during defrosting.	Use as required or cook for 5 (7) mins
Sausagemeat	400g (1lb)	4 (5) mins	6 (7) mins	10 mins	10 mins	Break thawed sausagemeat up and remove from oven during defrosting.	Use as required
Sausages	400g (1lb)	3–4 (4–5) mins	6 (7) mins	10 mins	10 mins	Separate during defrosting.	9 (11) mins
Bacon	200g (8oz)	2–3 (3–4) mins	4 (5) mins	5 mins	5 mins	Separate rashers during defrosting.	5–6 (6–7) mins
Lamb chops	2 100g (4oz)	2–3 (3–4) mins	4 (5) mins	5 mins	5 mins	Separate chops during defrosting.	4–5 (5–6) mins
Pork chops	2 200g (8oz)	3–4 (4–5) mins	6–7 (7–8) mins	10 mins	10 mins	Separate chops during defrosting.	10–11 (11–12) mins
Chicken portions	1 250–325g (10–13oz)	3–4 (4–5) mins	7 (8) mins	10 mins	10 mins	If necessary protect with aluminium foil during cooking.	5–7 (7–9) mins

Glazed Gammon

Method

1 Soak the gammon in cold water for 24 hours, changing the water occasionally if necessary. Dry well and weigh the joint.
2 Tie the joint securely with string. Score the fat with a sharp knife, making a diamond pattern.
3 Stand the joint on an inverted plate in a large dish. Cover the top with greased, greaseproof paper and cook for half the total cooking time, allowing 6–7 (7–8) minutes per 400g (1lb). Stand for 30 minutes.
4 Whilst the joint is standing, heat the orange juice and honey together for 2 (3) minutes.
5 After the 30 minutes standing time, brush the fat with the syrup and roll the gammon in 100g (4oz) of the sugar.
6 Return the gammon to the dish, turn over and finish cooking the joint for the required time.

Ingredients

1 unsmoked gammon, weighing about 3kg (6lb)
juice of 1 orange
3 15ml (tbsp) clear honey
150g (6oz) demerara sugar
mandarin segments or pineapple pieces for garnish

Power Level

Full (100%)

✳ ✳ ✳ ✳

7 Remove the joint from the cooker. Add the remaining sugar to the orange and honey mixture and cook the syrup for 3 (4) minutes, stirring once during cooking. Brush the fat with the glaze and leave to cool.
8 Decorate the gammon with mandarin segments and pineapple pieces on short, wooden cocktail sticks. Serve cold.

Rabbit Chasseur

Method

1 Toss the rabbit pieces in the flour. Melt the butter and oil together in a large dish for 1 (1½) minutes. Cook the rabbit, flesh side downwards, in the butter for 3 (4) minutes. Turn the pieces over and cook for 2 (3) minutes.
2 Remove the rabbit pieces and cook the vegetables in the butter for 2 (3) minutes. Stir once during the cooking time. Stir in the flour and add all the other ingredients slowly, stirring well.
3 Return the rabbit pieces to the casserole and cook, covered, for 15 (20) minutes.

Ingredients

4 rabbit portions
25g (1oz) plain flour
50g (2oz) butter
1 15ml (tbsp) oil
1 onion, chopped
2 carrots, peeled and sliced
100g (4oz) button mushrooms, washed
200ml (8fl oz) dry white wine
200ml (8fl oz) chicken stock
2 5ml (tsp) tomato purée
1 5ml (tsp) dried thyme
1 bay leaf
salt and pepper

Power Level

Full (100%)

✳ ✳ ✳ ✳

Serves 4

Turkey Meat Loaf

Method

1 Mince the meat and onion together and place in a large mixing bowl. Add all the other ingredients and mix thoroughly.

2 Press the mixture into a rectangular dish and cook in the microwave for 12–15 (17–20) minutes. Turn the dish every 5 minutes and allow 5 minutes standing time halfway through cooking

3 Serve hot or cold.

Ingredients

400g (1lb) cooked turkey meat
1 large onion
100g (4oz) breadcrumbs
3 15ml (tbsp) tomato purée
4 eggs
½ 5ml (tsp) allspice
pinch of nutmeg
salt and pepper

Power Level

Full (100%)

Serves 4–6

Spaghetti Bolognaise

Method

1 Heat the oil in a large bowl for 2 (2½) minutes. Add the onion, garlic, celery and carrot and cook for 3 (4) minutes.

2 Add the bacon and cook for 2 (3) minutes then add the minced beef, stir well and cook for 2 (3) minutes.

3 Stir in all the remaining ingredients, except the spaghetti and cheese, seasoning well. Cook for 10 (12) minutes, stir, cook for 10 (12) minutes. Adjust seasoning to taste. Serve with freshly cooked spaghetti, and grated Parmesan cheese.

Note

1 The bolognaise sauce is suitable for freezing.

2 The bolognaise sauce can be cooked for 10 (12) minutes on full (100%), left to stand for 10 minutes, then cooked for 20 (25) minutes on 50% setting.

Ingredients

2 15ml (tbsp) oil
1 onion, chopped
2 cloves garlic, finely chopped
2 sticks celery, finely chopped
1 carrot, diced
4 rashers streaky bacon, diced
400g (1lb) minced beef
½ green pepper, diced
4 tomatoes, skinned and chopped
250ml (½pt) boiling stock
2 15ml (tbsp) tomato purée
1 bay leaf
1 5ml (tsp) mixed herbs
pinch of nutmeg
salt and pepper
cooked spaghetti (see 'Vegetables')
2–3 15ml (tbsp) grated Parmesan cheese

Power Level

Full (100%) or 50%

Serves 4

Chilli con Carne

Method

1 Heat the oil in a large bowl for 2 (2½) minutes. Add the onions and cook for 3 (4) minutes. Add the meat and mix well.
2 Cook for 2 (3) minutes, stir, cook for 2 (3) minutes. Add the tomato purée and seasonings, mixing well.
3 Strain the kidney beans, reserving the juice and making up to 200ml (8fl oz) with water. Add the liquid to the meat.
4 Cook for 10 (12) minutes, stand for 5 minutes. Stir in the kidney beans then cook for 5–10 (10–15) minutes. Skim off the surplus fat and adjust the seasoning before serving.

Ingredients

2 15ml (tbsp) oil
2 large onions, finely chopped
400g (1lb) minced beef
2 15ml (tbsp) tomato purée
1–2 15ml (tbsp) chilli powder
1 5ml (tsp) paprika
salt and pepper
1 397g (14oz) can kidney beans

Power Level
Full (100%)

✳✳✳✳

Serves 4–6

Moussaka

Method

1 Melt the butter in a casserole dish for 1 (1½) minutes. Add the onions to the butter and cook, uncovered, for 2 (4) minutes. Add the meat, stir, and cook for 3–4 (6–7) minutes.
2 Stir in the tomatoes, tomato purée, stock or water and salt.
3 Cook the aubergines (see 'Vegetable Chart' page 90).
4 Fill a large glass or pottery dish with alternate layers of meat mixture and the aubergines. Sprinkle the wine over the moussaka.
5 Add the beaten egg and half the cheese to the basic white sauce. Stir well and adjust seasoning to taste. Pour the sauce over the moussaka and sprinkle the rest of the cheese on top.
6 Cook, uncovered, for 20–25 (25–30) minutes, turning the dish halfway through the cooking time.

Note

Cooked, sliced potatoes can be used instead of the aubergines if preferred.

Ingredients

400g (1lb) minced lamb or beef
25g (1oz) butter
200g (8oz) onions, finely chopped
200g (8oz) tomatoes, skinned and chopped
2 15ml (tbsp) tomato purée
2 15ml (tbsp) stock or water
1 5ml (tsp) salt
600g (1½lb) aubergines, thinly sliced
4 15ml (tbsp) white wine
1 egg, beaten
4 15ml (tbsp) grated Parmesan cheese
250ml (½pt) white sauce (see page 56)

Power Level
Full (100%)

Serves 4–6

Lamb with Dill Sauce

Method

1 Remove the meat from the bone and cut into 2cm (¾in) cubes. Place the meat in a casserole dish with the stock. Cover and cook for 5 (8) minutes.

2 Add the prepared vegetables, seasoning and 2 15ml (tbsp) dill. Cover and continue cooking for 10 (12) minutes. Allow to stand for 10 minutes then cook for a further 10 (12) minutes.

3 Melt the butter for 2 (2½) minutes, add the flour and gradually blend in the stock, drained from the meat and vegetables.

4 Cook the sauce for 5 (7) minutes, stirring 3 times during cooking. Add the vinegar and sugar and season to taste.

5 Blend the cream and egg yolk and beat into the sauce. Stir in the other 1 15ml (tbsp) of dill.

6 Combine the sauce, meat and vegetables in the casserole, mixing thoroughly. Cover and reheat, in the microwave, for 5 (7) minutes.

Ingredients

1.4kg (3lb) leg of lamb
500ml (1pt) stock
2 onions, sliced
200g (8oz) carrots, peeled and sliced
salt and pepper
2 15ml (tbsp) dried dill
50g (2oz) butter
50g (2oz) plain flour
2 15ml (tbsp) white wine vinegar
1 15ml (tbsp) sugar
4 15ml (tbsp) single cream
1 egg yolk
1 15ml (tbsp) dried dill

Power Level

Full (100%)

Serves 4

Armenian Lamb with Pilaf

Method

1 Cut the meat from the bone and divide into small cubes, about 2cm (¾in) square.

2 Melt the butter in a dish for 2 (2½) minutes, add the onion and garlic, cook for 3 (4) minutes. Add the meat, to the onion and garlic and cook, covered, for 2 (3) minutes.

3 Add all the other ingredients. Cook, covered, for 10 (12) minutes, stand for 15 minutes, cook for 5 (7) minutes.

For the Pilaf

1 Melt the butter in a large shallow dish for 2 (2½) minutes. Add the onion and rice and cook for 3 (5) minutes.

2 Add the stock and seasoning and cook, uncovered, for 12–15 (15–18) minutes, adding extra stock if necessary.

3 Carefully fork in the currants and nuts before serving with the lamb.

Ingredients

1kg (2lb) fillet end leg of lamb
40g (1½oz) butter
2 medium-sized onions, chopped
1 clove garlic, chopped
25g (1oz) plain flour
1 5ml (tsp) ground cumin seed
½ 5ml (tsp) ground allspice
2 15ml (tbsp) tomato purée
250ml (½pt) stock
salt and pepper

For the Pilaf

40g (1½oz) butter
1 small onion, chopped
200g (8oz) long grain rice
375ml (¾pt) chicken stock

salt and pepper
75g (3oz) currants
75g (3oz) pistachio nuts or almonds, blanched and shredded

Power Level

Full (100%)

Serves 4

Spare Ribs Sweet and Sour

Method

1. Place the spare ribs in a large shallow dish. Cook for 3 (5) minutes. Remove the chops from the dish and reserve.
2. Melt the butter in the dish for 1 (1½) minutes. Add the onion and cook for 3 (4) minutes. Stir in the flour then add the other ingredients, stirring the liquids in gradually.
3. Add the chops to the sauce. Cook, covered, for 5 (8) minutes.
4. Turn the chops and stir the sauce then return to the microwave and cook, uncovered, for 8–10 (10–12) minutes.

Ingredients

600g (1½lb) spare rib chops
250ml (½pt) chicken stock, boiling
25g (1oz) butter
25g (1oz) onion, chopped
25g (1oz) plain flour
25g (1oz) green pepper, deseeded and chopped
3 15ml (tbsp) crushed pineapple
1 15ml (tbsp) wine vinegar
2 15ml (tbsp) Worcestershire sauce
25g (1oz) soft brown sugar
1 15ml (tbsp) tomato purée
salt and pepper

Power Level

Full (100%)

✱✱✱✱

Serves 2–3

Hungarian Goulash

Method

1. Toss the meat in the seasoned flour. Heat the oil, in a large dish for 1–2 (3–4) minutes.
2. Stir in the meat then add all the other ingredients, blending well.
3. Cover and cook for 10 (14) minutes, stand for 10 minutes then cook for 15 (18) minutes. Remove bouquet garni before serving.

Note

Alternatively, the dish can be cooked for 10 (14) minutes on full, (100%), left to stand for 10 minutes, then cooked for 20 (25) minutes on 50% setting. This gives extra time for the flavours to blend.

Ingredients

400g (1lb) stewing steak, cut into small cubes
3 15ml (tbsp) seasoned flour
25ml (1fl oz) oil
2 medium-sized onions, chopped
1 green pepper, deseeded and chopped
2 5ml (tsp) paprika pepper
3 5ml (tsp) tomato purée
pinch of grated nutmeg
salt and pepper
50g (2oz) plain flour
250–375ml (½–¾pt) boiling stock
2 tomatoes, skinned and quartered
bouquet garni

Power Level

Full (100%) or 50%

Serves 4

Pork with Apricots and Prunes

Method

1 Heat the oil in a large, shallow casserole dish for 2 (2½) minutes. Add the prepared carrot and onion and cook for 3 (4) minutes.

2 Add the pork, cook for 3 (5) minutes, stir and cook for 2 (3) minutes.

3 Strain the apricot and prune juices into a measuring jug. Add the stock cube and make the juices up to 500ml (1pt) with boiling water. Add the sherry.

4 Season the meat well, add the liquid and half the apricots and prunes. Cover and cook for 15 (18) minutes. Stand for 10 minutes then cook for 10 (12) minutes.

5 Blend the cornflour with a little water and stir into the casserole. Cook for 3 (4) minutes, or until boiling.

6 Add the rest of the apricots and prunes. Cook for 2 (3) minutes and adjust seasoning if necessary, before serving.

Ingredients
2 15ml (tbsp) oil
1 carrot, sliced
1 onion, chopped
400g (1lb) lean pork, diced
1 212g (7½oz) can apricots
1 212g (7½oz) can prunes
1 chicken stock cube
1 15ml (tbsp) sherry
salt and black pepper
1 15ml (tbsp) cornflour

Power Level
Full (100%)

Serves 4

Shepherd's Pie

Method

1 Place the onion in a medium sized dish with the stock and cook for 4 (5) minutes.

2 Add the sauce, nutmeg, breadcrumbs, seasoning and meat, mixing thoroughly.

3 Mash the potato, add the butter and egg. Beat well and place on top of the meat. Smooth the top and heat through in the microwave for 10–15 (15–20) minutes.

Note

400g (1lb) of fresh meat could be used in the recipe instead of cooked meat. Cook the meat with the onion, sauce, nutmeg, breadcrumbs and seasoning, in the stock for 15 minutes. Thicken with 15g (½oz) plain flour. Finish the dish as above.

Ingredients
1 onion, chopped
250ml (½pt) boiling stock
1–2 15ml (tbsp) Worcestershire sauce
pinch of nutmeg
1 15ml (tbsp) breadcrumbs
salt and pepper
300g (12oz) cooked minced meat
400g (1lb) cooked potato
25g (1oz) butter
beaten egg

Power Level
Full (100%)

Serves 4

Liver Pâté

Method

1 Mince the livers, bread, onion and fat. Stir in all the other ingredients.

2 Grease a suitable deep round dish. Pile the pâté mixture into the dish and press down firmly.

3 Cook on 50% for 10 (14) minutes, stand for 5 minutes, cook on 50% for 5 (8) minutes. Allow to cool slightly then cover and place weights on top of the pâté. Leave in the refrigerator overnight. Turn out and garnish before serving.

Ingredients

300g (12oz) lamb's liver
50g (2oz) chicken livers
1 slice bread
1 small onion
100g (4oz) pork fat
½ 5ml (tsp) garlic salt
½ 5ml (tsp) ground black pepper
1 5ml (tsp) mixed herbs
1 5ml (tsp) lemon juice
1 egg
75ml (3fl oz) 'Bon' red wine
gherkin, tomato, juniper berries or olives for garnish.

Power Level

50%

Serves 8–12

Kidney and Bacon Casserole

Method

1 Halve the kidneys lengthwise and remove the core. Season the flour with gravy powder, herbs, garlic, salt and pepper. Toss the kidneys in the flour.

2 Heat the oil in a large casserole dish for 1 (1½) minutes. Add the onion and bacon and cook for 2 (3) minutes. Add the kidneys, cover and cook for 2 (3) minutes.

3 Add the carrot. Drain the tomatoes, reserving the juice. Crumble the stock cube into the tomato juice and make the liquid up to 250ml (½pt) with boiling water.

4 Add the tomatoes, liquid and Worcestershire sauce to the casserole. Cook, still covered for 10 (12) minutes, stand for 5 minutes. Add the mushrooms, replace the lid and cook for 5 (7) minutes.

5 Blend the cornflour with a little water then stir into the casserole and cover. Cook for 3 (4) minutes, or until boiling. Sprinkle with parsley before serving.

Ingredients

400g (1lb) lamb's kidneys
1 15ml (tbsp) plain flour
2 5ml (tsp) gravy powder
1 5ml (tsp) mixed herbs
pinch of garlic granules
salt and pepper
1 15ml (tbsp) oil
1 onion, chopped
4 rashers streaky bacon, diced
1 carrot, thinly sliced
1 396g (14oz) can tomatoes
1 stock cube
dash of Worcestershire sauce
100g (4oz) mushrooms, sliced
1 15ml (tbsp) cornflour
1 15ml (tbsp) chopped parsley

Power Level

Full (100%)

Serves 4

Quick Poor Man's Cassoulet

Method

1 Melt the lard in a large casserole for 2–3 (3–4) minutes. Add the garlic and pork strips. Cook for 2 (4) minutes then add the lamb and stock and cook for 2 (4) minutes.
2 Add the sausage, beans and brandy, if used. Season and stir well.
3 Cook for 10 (12) minutes, stand for 5 minutes, cook for 10 (12) minutes. Sprinkle with parsley before serving.

Ingredients
40g (1½oz) lard
2 large cloves garlic, finely chopped
4 pork strips, boned, trimmed and diced
150–200g (6–8oz) stewing lamb, diced
125ml (¼pt) chicken stock
200g (8oz) garlic or pork sausage, cut into 1.5cm (½in) cubes
2 425g (15oz) cans baked beans
2 15ml (tbsp) brandy (optional)
salt and pepper
1 15ml (tbsp) chopped parsley, for garnish
fresh bread to serve

Power Level
Full (100%)

Serves 6–8

Mexican Chicken

Method

1 Melt the butter in a large casserole dish for 1 (1½) minutes.
2 Add the peppers, onions, garlic and seasoning then cover with cling wrap and cook for 3 (5) minutes. Mix the tomatoes and tomato purée into the pepper mixture.
3 Season the chicken joints lightly and add to the pepper mixture. Cover and cook for 15 (17) minutes.
4 Add the sweetcorn and mushrooms and cook, still covered, for a further 15–20 (20–25) minutes.
5 Remove the chicken joints from the casserole. Stir the cream into the sauce and return the chicken to the casserole dish. Sprinkle with parsley before serving.

Ingredients
4 chicken portions
25g (1oz) butter
1 green pepper, deseeded and sliced
1 red pepper, deseeded and sliced
2 medium-sized onions, chopped
2 cloves garlic, crushed
salt and pepper
1 396g (14oz) can tomatoes
2 15ml (tbsp) tomato purée
100g (4oz) sweetcorn
100g (4oz) mushrooms, washed and sliced
4 15ml (tbsp) single cream
2 15ml (tbsp) chopped parsley

Power Level
Full (100%)

Serves 4

Chicken with Peanuts

Method

1 Toss the chicken joints in the seasoned flour. Heat the oil in a large dish for 1 (1½) minutes, add the onion and cook, covered, for 3 (4) minutes.

2 Add the chicken joints, flesh side downwards, and cook, uncovered, for 3 (4) minutes. Turn the joints over and cook for 2 (4) minutes.

3 Mix the milk, stock and peanut butter in a small bowl and heat for 2 (3) minutes. Pour over the chicken joints, cover and cook for 15 (20) minutes. Turn the dish every 5 minutes.

4 Remove the chicken pieces and blend the cornflour with a little of the sauce. Stir the cornflour into the liquid and cook for 4 (5) minutes, stirring every minute. Add the cream and seasoning and mix well.

5 Return the chicken to the dish, spooning the sauce over the joints. Reheat in the microwave for 3 (3½) minutes. Sprinkle with the peanuts and serve immediately.

Ingredients
4 chicken joints
2 15ml (tbsp) seasoned flour
2 15ml (tbsp) oil
1 onion, chopped
125ml (¼pt) milk
125ml (¼pt) stock
1 15ml (tbsp) peanut butter
1 15ml (tbsp) cornflour
2 15ml (tbsp) single cream
salt and pepper
50g (2oz) salted peanuts

Power Level
Full (100%)

Serves 4

Duck in Orange and Ginger Sauce

Method

1 Heat the oil in a large casserole dish for 2 (2½) minutes. Add the onions and cook for 3 (4) minutes.

2 Add the duck portions and cook for 5 (7) minutes.

3 Grate the rind from the oranges. Squeeze the juice from 1½ of the oranges. Add the stock cube and make the juice up to 500ml (1pt) with boiling water.

4 Add the honey, ginger and seasoning to the liquid then pour over the duck. Sprinkle the orange rind over the duck and add the bay leaf.

5 Cover and cook for 20 (25) minutes, stand for 10 minutes, cook for 10–15 (15–20) minutes.

6 Blend the cornflour with a little water. Remove the duck portions from the casserole. Stir the cornflour into the sauce after skimming off the surplus fat and removing the bay leaf. Cook for 3 (4) minutes, or until boiling. Stir well.

7 Return the duck to the sauce and reheat for 2 (3) minutes. Before serving garnish with orange slices from the remaining ½ orange.

Ingredients
1 15ml (tbsp) oil
1 onion, chopped
4 portions of duckling
2 oranges
1 chicken stock cube
3 15ml (tbsp) clear honey
1½ 5ml (tsp) ground ginger
salt and pepper
1 bay leaf
1 15ml (tbsp) cornflour

Power Level
Full (100%)

✳✳✳✳

Serves 4

Scandinavian Risotto

Method

1. Melt the butter for 1 (1½) minutes in a large shallow dish. Add the vegetables and cook for 2 (3) minutes. Add the rice and cook for a further 2 (4) minutes, or until the rice has absorbed the butter.
2. Pour in the stock and add the raisins and seasoning. Cover and cook for 15–20 (20–25) minutes.
3. Cut the gammon into 5mm (¼in) cubes, drain the pineapple and add both to the risotto. Stand for 10 minutes before serving.

Ingredients

50g (2oz) butter
2 onions, chopped
1 stick celery, finely sliced
1 green pepper, deseeded and sliced
150g (6oz) long grain rice
500ml (1pt) chicken stock
50g (2oz) raisins
salt and pepper
200g (8oz) cooked gammon
1 227g (8oz) can pineapple pieces

Power Level

Full (100%)

Serves 4–6

Veal à la Marengo

Method

1. Heat the oil in a large casserole for 2 (2½) minutes. Add onion and garlic and cook for 3 (4) minutes. Add the meat and cook for 5 (7) minutes.
2. Strain the juice from the tomatoes into a measuring jug. Add the stock cube and make the liquid up to 375ml (¾pt) with boiling water.
3. Put the tomatoes into the casserole, pour the stock over then add the sherry, bay leaf and seasoning. Cover and cook for 20 (25) minutes, stand for 10 minutes and stir well.
4. Cook for 10 (12) minutes. Remove the bay leaf and add the mushrooms. Cover and cook for 5 (7) minutes. Adjust seasoning, stir in the parsley and serve immediately.

Ingredients

2 15ml (tbsp) oil
2 onions, thinly sliced
2 cloves garlic, finely chopped
600g (1½lb) stewing veal, diced
1 397g (14oz) can tomatoes
1 chicken stock cube
2 15ml (tbsp) sherry
1 bay leaf
salt and pepper
100g (4oz) button mushrooms, sliced
1 5ml (tsp) parsley, chopped

Power Level

Full (100%)

Serves 4

Sage and Onion Stuffing

Method

1. Melt the butter in a bowl for 1 (1½) minutes. Toss the onion in the butter and cook for 3 (4) minutes, or until soft.
2. Stir in the sage, breadcrumbs and seasoning, mixing well. Allow to cool then bind the stuffing with beaten egg.

Ingredients

50g (2oz) butter
400g (1lb) onions, chopped
2 5ml (tsp) dried sage
100g (4oz) breadcrumbs
salt and pepper
1 egg beaten

Power Level

Full (100%)

Serves 4

Walnut Stuffing

Method

1 Finely chop the walnuts and onion. Melt the butter in the microwave, for 1 (1½) minutes. Add the onion and cook for 3 (4) minutes.

2 Mix in the rest of the ingredients, using just enough beaten egg to bind the stuffing. Season well.

3 The stuffing can also be made by melting the butter for 1 (1½) minutes and then liquidising all the ingredients together. This gives a finely textured stuffing.

Ingredients
100g (4oz) walnuts
1 medium-sized onion
40g (1½oz) butter
40g (1½oz) breadcrumbs
1 15ml (tbsp) chopped parsley
1 5ml (tsp) dried marjoram
grated rind and juice of ½ lemon
1 egg, beaten
salt and pepper

Power Level
Full (100%)

Serves 4

Sweetcorn Stuffing

Method

1 Melt the butter, in the microwave, for 1 (1½) minutes. Toss the onion in the butter and cook for 3 (4) minutes.

2 Add the sweetcorn and seasoning and cook for 2 (3) minutes. Allow to cool.

3 Stir in the parsley, grated lemon rind, a little juice from the lemon and the breadcrumbs. Adjust the seasoning to taste then bind the stuffing with beaten egg.

Ingredients
25g (1oz) butter
1 onion, chopped
1 219g (7oz) can sweetcorn
salt and pepper
1 15ml (tbsp) chopped parsley
1 lemon
100g (4oz) breadcrumbs
1 egg, beaten

Power Level
Full (100%)

Serves 4

Orange and Herb Stuffing

Method

1 Melt the butter, in the microwave, for 1 (1½) minutes. Toss the onion in the butter and cook for 3 (4) minutes.

2 Add all the other ingredients, mixing well.

Ingredients
50g (2oz) butter
50g (2oz) onion, chopped
100g (4oz) breadcrumbs
grated rind and juice of 1 orange
1 15ml (tbsp) dried mixed herbs
salt and pepper
1 egg, beaten

Power Level
Full (100%)

Serves 4

Vegetables

Fresh vegetables from the microwave are delicious and retain their full flavour, colour and nutritional value, as they are cooked in their own juices requiring very little additional liquid. In fact some vegetables, spinach and spring greens, for example, are cooked using only the water which clings to the leaves after washing. We have found roasting bags and boiling bags ideal for cooking vegetables as they can be easily shaken or turned over to stir the contents during the cooking cycle. Remember, however, that the wire ties supplied with some makes must not be used; rubber bands or string ties make suitable alternatives and the bag should be tied loosely to allow some steam to escape. Vegetables will remain hot for a considerable time after cooking if the bag is not opened. It is, therefore, possible to cook several varieties of vegetables one after another and serve them together.

If preferred, vegetables may be cooked using more water in a casserole dish, covered with a lid or cling wrap, but the cooking time should be increased to allow for the extra volume in the oven. It is not always quicker to cook vegetables by microwave than cooking conventionally but the results are well worthwhile.

Points to Remember

Do not over season the vegetables as it can have a toughening effect. If in doubt, correct seasoning after cooking.

The times given are approximate as the age and the thickness of the vegetables will affect cooking time. Therefore, test regularly during cooking.

If the quantity given on the chart is altered, the time should be adjusted accordingly. Allow about ⅓–½ extra time if doubling the quantity of vegetables to be cooked.

Do not over cook as the vegetables will continue to cook for a short while after they are removed from the oven due to the heat retained.

Vegetables cooked in their skins, i.e. jacket potatoes and tomatoes should be pricked well to prevent the vegetables bursting during cooking.

When 'boiling' potatoes it is usually better to cook them in their skins with a little added water as described previously and to remove the skins, if required, after cooking. Some kinds of potatoes cook extremely well either scraped or peeled but some varieties tend to turn black during cooking in the microwave.

It is possible to blanch vegetables for the freezer in the microwave oven but only attempt small quantities at a time. Some vegetables are more successful and will keep a better colour than others, for example we have found during our tests that sprouts, although acceptable, were better for being blanched conventionally although cauliflower was most successful with very little difference between the two methods.

The vegetables should be prepared for blanching in the normal way, placed in a large covered casserole with water allowing 75–100ml (3–4fl oz) per 400g (1lb) vegetables, depending on the type, for example sliced runner beans would require slightly less water than cauliflower florets.

The vegetables should be cooked for half the recommended cooking time given on the vegetable cooking chart, but it is important to shake or stir the food at least once during the blanching period. After blanching, cool the vegetables in iced water, pack and freeze in the normal way. The vegetables should be cooked for the full time recommended for fresh vegetables but allow an extra 1–3 mins. if using them straight from the freezer, when no extra water will be required.

Vegetables may be blanched in boiling bags for convenience, with very little water – about as much as recommended when cooking vegetables. To blanch them, cook in the microwave for half the recommended cooking time, shaking them frequently throughout. Chill them by plunging into a bowl of iced water, still in the bag; this will reduce the temperature and the water will serve to expel the air in the bag, automatically creating a vacuum pack for the freezer. Seal the bag in the normal way and freeze.

8   Frozen vegetables may be cooked from frozen. They should be placed in a roasting bag, boiling bag or covered casserole dish and sprinkled with salt. It is not usually necessary to add any additional liquid unless preferred when extra time will be necessary to allow for the extra volume of water. For quantities up to ½kg (1lb) cook for the time recommended on the packet. For larger amounts increase the cooking time accordingly (⅓–½ extra time if doubling the quantity). During the cooking cycle it is important to separate any vegetables which are still frozen at the centre of the pack and to stir once more before cooking is complete.

9   Canned vegetables must be removed from the tin and placed into a suitable container. They may be heated with or without their liquor as preferred but if heating them drained, they should be covered with a lid or cling wrap and will take 1½–2 (2½–3) minutes for a 425g (15oz) can, depending on type.

Pasta and Rice

Although there is no particular time saving over cooking conventionally, microwave pasta and rice means no steaming kitchen or sticky saucepans. Good results can be obtained with no boiling over saucepans and with very little attention paid during cooking.

Instructions for cooking rice and pasta are given on the cooking chart on page 90.

Vegetable, Rice and Pasta Cooking Chart

Vegetable and Quantity	Preparation	Amount of Salted Water to be Added	Cooking Time on 'Full' (100%)	
Asparagus 200g (8oz)	Trim and leave whole	2 15ml (tbsp)	Thin spears 6–8 (7–9) minutes Thick spears 8–10 (9–11) minutes	
Aubergines 400g (1lb)	Wash, slice, sprinkle with salt and leave for 30 minutes. Rinse	2 15ml (tbsp)	8–10 (9–11) minutes	
Beetroot 400g (1lb)	Peel and slice	2 15ml (tbsp)	7–8 (8–9) minutes	
Brussels Sprouts 400g (1lb)	Wash, remove outer leaves and trim	2 15ml (tbsp)	8–10 (9–11) minutes	
Broccoli 400g (1lb)	Trim, cut into spears	2 15ml (tbsp)	8–12 (9–13) minutes	Cooking times will vary on thickness of spears
Cabbage 400g (1lb)	Wash and shred finely	2 15ml (tbsp)	8–10 (9–11) minutes	
Carrots 200g (8oz)	*New* – wash, scrape and cut into strips or leave whole, depending on size *Old* – scrape and slice	2 15ml (tbsp)	7–10 (9–11) minutes	
Cauliflower 600g (1½lb)	Wash and cut into florets	4 15ml (tbsp)	9–11 (11–13) minutes	
Celery 300g (12oz)	Wash, trim and slice	3 15ml (tbsp)	10–12 (12–14) minutes	
Corn on the cob 2 200g (8oz)	Wash and trim	4 15ml (tbsp)	8–10 (9–11) minutes	
Courgettes 400g (1lb)	Trim, slice and sprinkle with salt	—	8–10 (9–11) minutes	
Leeks 400g (1lb)	Trim, slice and sprinkle with salt	2 15ml (tbsp)	7–10 (9–12) minutes	
Marrow 400g (1lb)	Peel, cut into 2cm (¾in) rings, remove seeds and halve rings	2 15ml (tbsp)	8–10 (9–11) minutes	

Vegetable and Quantity	Preparation	Amount of Salted Water to be Added	Cooking Time on 'Full' (**100**%)	
Mushrooms 200g (8oz)	Peel or wash	2 15ml (tbsp) of stock	5–6 (6–7) minutes	
New Potatoes in their jackets 400g (1lb)	Wash thoroughly	2 15ml (tbsp)	10–12 (12–14) minutes	Use small, evenly sized potatoes
Parsnips 400g (1lb)	Peel and dice	2 15ml (tbsp)	8–10 (9–11) minutes	
Peas 200g (8oz)	Remove from pods	2 15ml (tbsp)	8–10 (9–11) minutes	
Runner beans 400g (1lb)	String and slice	2 15ml (tbsp)	8–10 (9–11) minutes	
Spinach 400g (1lb)	Break up thicker stalks, wash and sprinkle with salt	—	6–8 (7–9) minutes	
Spring greens 400g (1lb)	Break up thicker stalks, wash and sprinkle with salt	—	8–10 (9–11) minutes	
Swedes 400g (1lb)	Peel and dice	2 15ml (tbsp)	6–7 (7–8) minutes	
Tomatoes 400g (1lb)	Wash, halve, sprinkle with salt, place in shallow dish and cover with lid or cling wrap	—	6–8 (8–10) minutes	
Turnips 400g (1lb)	Peel and dice	2 15ml (tbsp)	8–10 (9–11) minutes	
American, long grain or Patna Rice 200g (8oz)	Place in deep covered dish, with salt and a large knob of butter	500ml (1pt) boiling water	10–12 (12–14) minutes	Stir after adding water. Leave to stand for 5–10 minutes until water is absorbed
Elbow macaroni, small pasta noodles 200g (8oz)	Place in deep dish with salt and 1 15ml (tbsp) oil	500ml (1pt) boiling water	10–15 (15–20) minutes, uncovered	Leave to stand for 10–15 minutes until pasta is swollen and most of water absorbed
Spaghetti 200g (8oz)	Break into half or thirds, place in long dish	500ml (1pt) boiling water	10–15 (15–20) minutes, uncovered	Leave to stand for 10–15 minutes, until pasta is swollen and most of water is absorbed

Vegetable Curry

Method
1 Melt the butter in a large, deep dish, for $1\frac{1}{2}$ (2) minutes. Cook the onion, garlic and apple in the butter for 3 (4) minutes.
2 Stir in the curry powder, flour and seasonings then cook for 1 minute.
3 Drain the juice from the tomatoes and beans into a measuring jug. Add the crumbled stock cube and make the liquid up to 500ml (1pt) with boiling water.
4 Gradually add the stock to the sauce base, beating well. Cook for 6 (8) minutes, stirring every 2 minutes.
5 Add the prepared vegetables, chutney and sultanas. Stir well, cover and cook for 5 (7) minutes on full (100%) then 30 (35) minutes on 50% setting.
6 Add the tomatoes and butter beans and cook for 5 (7) minutes on full (100%), before serving.

Note
The curry can be cooked for 20–25 (25–30) minutes on full (100%) before adding the tomatoes and butter beans and cooking for 5 (7) minutes on full (100%). Cooking on 50% simply allows more time for the rich curry flavours to blend.

Ingredients
50g (2oz) butter
1 large onion, chopped
2 cloves garlic, finely chopped
1 apple, peeled, cored and diced
2 15ml (tbsp) curry powder
2 15ml (tbsp) plain flour
1 5ml (tsp) allspice
salt and pepper
1 425g (15oz) can tomatoes
1 425g (15oz) can butter beans
1 stock cube
600–700g ($1\frac{1}{2}$–$1\frac{3}{4}$lb) prepared mixed vegetables, e.g. celery, cauliflower, carrots, aubergine, courgette
2 15ml (tbsp) chutney
50g (2oz) sultanas

Power Level
Full (100%) and 50%

Serves 6–8

Stuffed Peppers

Method
1 Cut a slice from the top of each of the peppers. Remove the core and seeds, reserving the slice to use as a lid.
2 Cook the peppers for 2 (3) minutes, turn and cook for 2 (3) minutes.
3 Put the rice, stock, onion, seasoning and bay leaf in a dish. Cover and cook for 5 (7) minutes, stir, cook for 3–5 (5–7) minutes, or until the stock is absorbed. Remove bay leaf.
4 Add the ham and sultanas to the rice. Carefully fill the peppers with the mixture and replace the lids.
5 Stand the peppers in a suitable dish and reheat for 3 (5) minutes.

Ingredients
2 medium-sized green peppers
50g (2oz) long grain rice
165ml ($\frac{1}{3}$pt) boiling stock
1 onion, finely chopped
salt and pepper
1 bay leaf
50g (2oz) cooked ham, chopped
40g ($1\frac{1}{2}$oz) sultanas

Power Level
Full (100%)

Serves 1 or 2

Ratatouille

Method

- Sprinkle the prepared aubergines and courgettes with salt. Stand for 30 minutes then wash thoroughly.
- Heat the oil in a large casserole for 4 (5) minutes. Add the onion and garlic and cook for 3 (5) minutes.
- Add the aubergines and courgettes and cook for 3 (5) minutes. Add the peppers, tomatoes and seasoning.
- Cover and cook for 20–25 (25–30) minutes, stirring once during the cooking time.

Ingredients

1–2 aubergines (depending on size), sliced
200g (8oz) courgettes, sliced
4 15ml (tbsp) oil
1 large onion, sliced
2 cloves garlic, finely chopped
1 red pepper, deseeded and finely sliced
1 green pepper, deseeded and finely sliced
200g (8oz) tomatoes, skinned, deseeded and roughly chopped
salt and pepper

Power Level

Full (100%)

✳ ✳ ✳ ✳

Serves 4–6

German Red Cabbage

Method

- Melt the butter in a large, shallow casserole dish for 1½ (2) minutes. Add the red cabbage and cook for 3 (5) minutes.
- Add all the remaining ingredients and stir well. Cover and cook for 20–25 (25–30) minutes, or until cooked.
- Remove bay leaf before serving.

Ingredients

50g (2oz) butter
400g (1lb) red cabbage, very finely shredded
2 onions, sliced
2 cloves garlic, finely chopped
1 cooking apple, diced
1 bay leaf
pinch each of parsley, thyme, cinnamon and nutmeg
salt and black pepper
grated rind of 1 orange
1 5ml (tsp) caraway seed
2 15ml (tbsp) soft brown sugar
1 small wine glass red wine

Power Level

Full (100%)

Serves 4–6

Casserole of Courgettes

Method

1 Place the courgettes, tomatoes, onion, garlic, vinegar and seasoning in a covered, ovenware casserole. Cook for 12–14 (14–16) minutes.
2 Stir in the parsley and sprinkle with grated cheese. Melt in the microwave for 3–5 (4–6) minutes or brown under a conventional grill.

Ingredients

200g (8oz) courgettes, trimmed and thinly sliced
200g (8oz) tomatoes, skinned and sliced
1 small onion, finely chopped
1 clove garlic, crushed
1 15ml (tbsp) vinegar
salt and pepper
2 5ml (tsp) chopped parsley
50g (2oz) cheese, finely grated

Power Level

Full (100%)

✱✶✶✶

Serves 4

Braised Celery

Method

1 Melt the butter for 1 (1½) minutes in a large shallow dish. Add the bacon and onion and cook for 2 (3) minutes.
2 Add the celery, stock and seasoning. Cover and cook for 15–20 (20–25) minutes.

Ingredients

25g (1oz) butter
2 rashers bacon, chopped
1 small onion, finely chopped
300g (12oz) celery, cut into 5–7.5cm (2–3in) lengths
250ml (½pt) stock
salt and pepper

Power Level

Full (100%)

Serves 4

Stuffed Marrow

Method

1 Melt the butter in a large bowl, for 1 (1½) minutes add onion and garlic and cook for 3 (4) minutes.
2 Add the mince and seasonings, cook for 2 (4) minutes, stir and cook for a further 2 (4) minutes.
3 Add the tomatoes, mushrooms and breadcrumbs, stir thoroughly and adjust seasoning to taste.
4 Arrange the marrow rings in a large casserole and fill the centre of each ring with the mince mixture. If necessary make a second layer of rings in the dish.
5 Cover and cook for 20–30 (25–35) minutes, turning once.

Ingredients

25g (1oz) butter
1 onion, chopped
1 clove garlic, finely chopped
400g (1lb) minced beef
salt and pepper
1 5ml (tsp) basil
dash of Worcestershire sauce
200g (8oz) tomatoes, skinned and chopped
50g (2oz) mushrooms, chopped
75g (3oz) breadcrumbs
1 marrow, peeled, deseeded and cut into 8 rings

Power Level

Full (100%)

Serves 4

Cauliflower Cheese

Method

Break the cauliflower into florets. Place them in a roasting bag with the salt and water. Loosely seal the neck of the bag and cook for 10–12 (12–14) minutes.

Season the white sauce with salt, cayenne and mustard. Stir in the cheese.

Lay the cauliflower in a suitable dish then spoon over the sauce. Reheat in the microwave for 3–5 (4–6) minutes. Garnish with the tomato and serve.

Variations

The following ingredients can be added to the sauce, in place of, or as well as the cheese. Cook as above.

75g (3oz) cooked bacon, chopped
75g (3oz) cooked onion, chopped

Ingredients

1 cauliflower, about 600g (1½lb) prepared weight
pinch of salt
4 15ml (tbsp) water
250ml (½pt) white sauce (see page 56)
pinch each of salt, cayenne pepper, dry mustard
75g (3oz) Cheddar cheese, grated
1 tomato, sliced

Power Level

Full (100%)

Serves 4–6

Swiss Tomato Casserole

Method

Place the butter, flour and milk in a bowl. Cook for 5–6 (6–7) minutes, stirring every minute, until the sauce is well thickened. Season and add the Gruyère cheese and cream or milk.

Arrange a layer of sliced tomatoes in the bottom of a casserole. Sprinkle with seasoning, a little basil and sugar. Spoon some of the sauce over the tomatoes.

Continue with these layers until all the ingredients are used up, finishing with a layer of sauce.

Sprinkel with Parmesan cheese, cover and cook for 10–12 (14–16) minutes.

Ingredients

40g (1½oz) butter
40g (1½oz) plain flour
375ml (¾pt) milk
salt and pepper
100g (4oz) Gruyère cheese, grated
4 15ml (tbsp) single cream or top of the milk
600g (1½lb) ripe, firm tomatoes, skinned and sliced
½ 5ml (tsp) basil
2 5ml (tsp) caster sugar
25g (1oz) grated Parmesan cheese

Power Level

Full (100%)

Serves 4–6

95

Jacket Potatoes

Method

1 Scrub the potatoes then dry and prick them with a fork or score them.
2 Cook for 10–12 (12–15) minutes, or until soft. Cut the potatoes in half and scoop out the soft potato.
3 Mix with the butter and seasoning, then pile the filling back into the potato skins. Reheat, in the microwave, for 1 (2) minutes.

Variations

Cheese: Add the following to the cooked potato and reheat as above.
  50g (2oz) cheese, grated
  15g (½oz) butter
  ½ 5ml (tsp) milk
Bacon: Add the following to the cooked potato and reheat as above.
  50g (2oz) cooked bacon, chopped
  ½ 5ml (tsp) milk
Soured Cream and Chives: Add the following to the cooked potato and reheat as above.
  2 15ml (tbsp) soured cream
  1 5ml (tsp) chives, chopped

Ingredients

2 potatoes (each 225–250g/9–10oz)
knob of butter
salt and pepper

Power Level

Full (100%)

Serves 2 or 4

Mushrooms au Gratin

Method

1 Melt the butter, in a suitable serving dish, for 1½ (2) minutes. Add the mushrooms, cover with cling wrap and cook for 5 (7) minutes. Season lightly.
2 Season the white sauce with mace and cayenne pepper then stir in the cream. Spoon the sauce over the mushrooms.
3 Sprinkle with breadcrumbs and cheese then reheat in the microwave for 2 (4) minutes.

Ingredients

25g (1oz) butter
400g (1lb) button mushrooms, sliced
salt and pepper
250ml (½pt) white sauce (see page 56)
pinch of mace
pinch of cayenne pepper
125ml (¼pt) single cream
3 15ml (tbsp) browned breadcrumbs
3 15ml (tbsp) Parmesan cheese, grated

Power Level

Full (100%)

Serves 4

Fruit and Sweets

Fresh fruit can be prepared in the normal way, sprinkled with sugar and cooked in a roasting bag or boiling bag in a similar manner to fresh vegetables. The fruit should be checked and stirred or turned regularly to make sure it does not overcook. When it is important that the fruit pieces do not break, cook them in a covered casserole when a little more liquid should be used and the cooking time increased accordingly to account for the extra volume in the oven. Fruits cooked in their skins such as baked apples should be pricked or scored to prevent the fruits from bursting during the cooking process. As most fruit can be cooked with no additional liquid, they can soon be sieved or puréed to make sauces to pour over ice cream, natural yoghurt or puddings.

Even those favourite jam and syrup puddings that are almost a thing of the past because of their length of steaming time, are available again with microwave cooking in just a fraction of the time. Jellies for trifles and gelatine for mousses can be melted in seconds and fresh fruit in wine or liqueur can be quickly prepared for a really delicious simple sweet. The range of desserts which may be prepared or cooked by microwave is almost never ending, the advantage being that they can be made in advance and served cold, or reheated when required, in individual portions if necessary, according to your family's preference.

When cooking sponge puddings, take the dish from the oven whilst it is still very lightly moist as cooking will continue and the pudding will 'set' during its standing time. You may care to read the next section on 'Cakes' as some of the same cooking techniques apply.

When thawing out a frozen dessert it should be given short bursts of microwave energy, followed by a standing or heat equalization period. Repeat the process until thawed and the food is at an even temperature throughout.

Fruit Cooking Chart

Fruit and Quantity	Preparation	Cooking Time on 'Full' (100%)	Cooking Time on 50% setting
Apricots 400g (1lb)	Stone and wash. Sprinkle with sugar to taste.	6–8 (8–10) minutes	11–15 (13–18) minutes
Cooking apples 400g (1lb)	Peel, core and slice. Sprinkle with sugar to taste.	6–8 (8–10) minutes	11–15 (13–18) minutes
Gooseberries 400g (1lb)	Top and tail, sprinkle with sugar.	4–5 (5–6) minutes	7–8 (9–10) minutes
Peaches 4 medium-sized	Stone and wash. Sprinkle with sugar.	4–5 (5–6) minutes	7–8 (9–10) minutes
Pears 6 medium-sized	Peel, halve and core. Dissolve 75g (3oz) sugar and a pinch of cinnamon in a little hot water. Pour over the pears.	8–10 (10–12) minutes	15–20 (20–25) minutes
Plums 400g (1lb)	Stone and wash. Sprinkle with sugar to taste and add grated rind of ½ lemon.	4–5 (5–6) minutes	7–8 (9–10) minutes
Rhubarb 400g (1lb)	Trim, wash and cut into short lengths. Add 100g (4oz) sugar and grated rind of 1 lemon.	7–10 (9–12) minutes	14–20 (18–24) minutes
Soft fruits, e.g. blackcurrants, redcurrants, loganberries, blackberries, etc. 400g (1lb)	Top and tail currants, hull the berries. Wash well. Add sugar to taste.	3–5 (4–6) minutes	6–10 (8–12) minutes

Bread and Butter Pudding

Method

Butter the bread, remove the crusts and cut the slices in half diagonally.

Arrange the bread in layers in a 750ml (1½pt) pie dish, sprinkling each layer with sultanas.

Beat the eggs with the sugar then mix with the milk and vanilla essence. Pour the custard over the bread.

Stand the pie dish in a shallow water bath in the microwave. Cook for 5 (8) minutes, stand for 5 minutes, turn and cook for 5 (8) minutes, or until custard sets in the centre.

The top of the pudding can be crisped under a hot grill if desired before serving.

Note

The size of the water bath and the depth of the water in it will affect the cooking time slightly.

Ingredients

6 large slices bread, white or brown
75g (3oz) butter
50g (2oz) sultanas
3 eggs
40g (1½oz) caster sugar
375ml (¾pt) milk
few drops vanilla essence

Power Level

Full (100%)

Serves 4

Christmas Pudding

Method

Grease either 3 500ml (1pt) or 2 750ml (1½pt) pudding basins. Mix all the dry ingredients together in a large bowl then add the other ingredients, mixing thoroughly.

Divide the mixture between the basins and cover with cling wrap, making 2 slits in the top.

Cook each 500ml (1pt) pudding for 5 (8) minutes then stand for 10 minutes before turning out. Cook each 750ml (1½pt) pudding for 6–7 (8–9) minutes, then stand for 10 minutes before turning out.

Ingredients

125g (5oz) plain flour
1 15ml (tbsp) mixed spice
150g (6oz) breadcrumbs
200g (8oz) soft brown sugar
200g (8oz) suet
500g (1¼lb) mixed dried fruit
100g (4oz) mixed chopped peel
grated rind of 1 orange
1 medium-sized eating apple, peeled and grated
4 eggs
3 15ml (tbsp) black treacle
1 15ml (tbsp) malt extract
2 15ml (tbsp) milk
125ml (¼pt) stout

Power Level

Full (100%)

Serves about 12

Fruit and Nut Pudding

Method

1 Place all the ingredients in a large bowl and mix thoroughly. Beat for 5 minutes.
2 Divide the mixture and place in 2 750ml (1½pt) greased pudding basins. Cover with cling wrap, and make two slits in the top.
3 Cook each pudding for 7–9 (9–11) minutes then leave to stand for 5 minutes. Serve with custard or cream.

Ingredients

2 large cooking apples, peeled and finely chopped
50g (2oz) raisins
50g (2oz) walnuts, chopped
100g (4oz) butter
200g (8oz) brown sugar
2 eggs
200ml (8fl oz) milk
200g (8oz) plain flour
1 5ml (tsp) baking powder
½ 5ml (tsp) salt
pinch of ground cloves
½ 5ml (tsp) nutmeg
2 5ml (tsp) cinnamon

Power Level

Full (100%)

Serves 8–12

Sponge Pudding

Method

1 Grease a 1l (2pt) pudding basin. Cream the butter and sugar in a mixing bowl, until light and fluffy.
2 Gradually beat in the eggs. Stir in the flour and vanilla essence then turn the mixture into the prepared basin.
3 Cook in the microwave for 5 (6) minutes or 6 (7) minutes if making one of the variations.

Variations

Syrup – Place 3 15ml (tbsp) of golden syrup in the bottom of the basin. Add mixture and cook as above.

Jam – Place 3 15ml (tbsp) of jam in the bottom of the basin. Add mixture and cook as above.

Pineapple – Arrange 5 pineapple rings in the prepared basin. Put a glacé cherry in the centre of each ring then add the mixture and cook as above.

Sultana – Stir 50–75g (2–3oz) of dried fruit into the sponge mixture. Cook as above.

Ingredients

100g (4oz) butter
100g (4oz) caster sugar
2 eggs
100g (4oz) self-raising flour
few drops of vanilla essence

Power Level

Full (100%)

Serves 4

Oranges in Caramel

Method

Finely grate the rind of 3 of the oranges. Remove the peel and outer membrane from all the oranges.

Hold the oranges over a serving dish. Slice the oranges, holding each one together with a wooden cocktail stick.

Stir the sugar into the cold water with the liqueur, if used. Bring to the boil in the microwave, without stirring and boil until a light golden brown. (approximately 10–12 (14–16) minutes.)

Quickly add the warm water to the caramel, protecting your hand from the steam with a towel. Return to the microwave for 30 (45) seconds. Stir well and leave to cool.

Pour the cooled caramel over the oranges, in the serving dish and sprinkle with the grated orange rind. Chill well before serving.

Ingredients

8 oranges
200g (8oz) granulated sugar
125ml (¼pt) cold water
1 5ml (tsp) Grand Marnier (optional)
125ml (¼pt) warm water

Power Level

Full (100%)

✳ ✱ ✱ ✱

Serves 4–6

Apple and Raspberry Suet Pudding

Method

Place the flour and suet together in a mixing bowl. Mix to a soft, manageable dough with cold water.

Grease a 750ml (1½pt) pudding basin and line with ⅔ of the suet pastry.

Layer the filling into the lined basin and roll out the remaining pastry to a circle to fit the top of the pudding. Damp and seal the edges.

Cover the top of the basin with cling wrap, very tightly. Invert the basin and cook for 2 (3) minutes.

Turn the pudding the right way up and snip the cling wrap completely away from the top of the pudding.

Cook for 5 (6) minutes, turn, cook for 5 (6) minutes.

Ingredients

For the suet crust
200g (8oz) self-raising flour
150g (6oz) shredded suet
water, to mix
For the filling
400–600g (1–1½lb) cooking apples, peeled, cored and sliced
100g (4oz) caster sugar
1 425g (15oz) can raspberries, drained

Power Level

Full (100%)

✳ ✱ ✱ ✱

Serves 4–6

Cheesecake

Method

1 Line a 20cm (8in) flan dish with cling wrap. Melt the butter in the dish for 1½–2 (2–2½) minutes. Stir in the biscuit crumbs and the sugar. Press the mixture evenly over the base of the dish, using a metal spoon.
2 Beat the cheese until smooth, add the sugar and beat again. Gradually add the eggs and finally the vanilla essence.
3 Pour the filling onto the base and cook for 7–10 (9–12) minutes, turning every 2–3 minutes.
4 Leave to cool. Chill for 1 hour then spoon the fruit topping over the filling before serving.

Variation

Omit the vanilla essence, adding
grated zest of 1 lemon
50g (2oz) mixed peel
50g (2oz) sultanas
to the filling instead. Cook as above. Omit the fruit topping, use lemon jelly if required.

Note

The cheesecake can be cooked for 25–30 (30–35) minutes on 50% setting, turning 3–4 times, until set.

Ingredients

For the base
75g (3oz) butter
150g (6oz) digestive biscuits, crushed
2 5ml (tsp) caster sugar

For the filling
400g (1lb) cream cheese
75g (3oz) caster sugar
2 eggs
2 5ml (tsp) vanilla essence

For the topping
1 347g (14oz) can fruit pie filling, any flavour

Power Level

Full (100%) or 50%

Serves 6–8

Chocolate Semolina Pudding

Method

1 Bring milk to the boil in a 1l (2pt) pie dish. This will take approximately 5 (8) minutes.
2 Add the semolina, sugar and butter, stir.
3 Cook for 5 (7) minutes until thick, stirring frequently.
4 Add the chocolate and stir until melted.

Ingredients

500ml (1pt) milk
40g (1½oz) semolina or ground rice
50g (2oz) caster sugar
15g (½oz) butter
50g (2oz) chocolate, broken into squares

Power Level

Full (100%)

Serves 4

Apfel Strudel

Method

- Prepare the paste. Place the flour and the salt in a bowl, add the eggs, oil and lemon juice. Beat the mixture vigorously until it leaves the sides of the bowl.
- Cover and leave in a warm place for 30 minutes.
- Melt the butter for 1½ (2) minutes then stir in the breadcrumbs. In a separate bowl mix the apple and lemon rind.
- Roll half the strudel paste out on a clean, lightly floured tea towel, to give a large, thin rectangle.
- Brush the paste with oil and spread half the jam over this. Sprinkle with half the breadcrumbs then half the apple and lemon mixture.
- Finally add half the sultanas, almonds, sugar and cinnamon. Fold over about 2.5cm (1in) of the paste on each of the shorter sides and brush with water.
- Roll up the strudel, starting from a long edge and using the tea towel to help. Dampen the other long edge and seal.
- Repeat stages 4–7 with the rest of the paste and filling. Cook the 2 strudels together on kitchen paper in the microwave, for 8 (10) minutes, turning halfway through the cooking time, or cook separately for 5 (6½) minutes each.
- Dredge with icing sugar and slice before serving hot or cold.

Ingredients

For the paste
200g (8oz) plain flour
pinch of salt
2 eggs
2 15ml (tbsp) oil
juice of 2 lemons

For the filling
50g (2oz) butter
50g (2oz) breadcrumbs
grated rind of 2 lemons
1kg (2lb) cooking apples, peeled and shredded
1 15ml (tbsp) oil
4 15ml (tbsp) red jam, sieved
75g (3oz) sultanas
100g (4oz) ground almonds
75g (3oz) brown sugar
2 5ml (tsp) cinnamon
icing sugar, for dredging

Power Level
Full (100%)

✱✱✱✱

Serves 8–10

Fruit Crumble

Method

- Prepare the fruit then place in the bottom of a pie dish with the caster sugar.
- Sift the flour into a bowl and rub in the butter. Stir in most of the demerara sugar.
- Sprinkle the mixture over the fruit and top with the remaining demerara sugar.
- Cook for 10–12 (14–16) minutes, turning the dish halfway through the cooking time.

Ingredients

600g (1½lb) fresh or canned fruit (use 800g (2lb) if the fruit has to be stoned)
100g (4oz) caster sugar
150g (6oz) plain flour
75g (3oz) butter
50g (2oz) demerara sugar

Power Level
Full (100%)

Serves 4

103

Stuffed Baked Apples

Method

1 Core the apples but do not peel. Score the fruit and place in individual dishes or in a suitable serving dish.
2 Fill the centre of each apple with a mixture of sugar, currants and lemon juice.
3 Pour 2 5ml (tsp) of golden syrup over each apple.
4 Cover the fruit with greased, greaseproof paper and cook for 4–5 (6–7) minutes.

Note

Cook 1 apple for 2–3 (4–5) minutes.
Cook 4 apples for 6–8 (9–11) minutes.

Ingredients

2 medium-sized cooking apples
brown sugar
currants
lemon juice
4 5ml (tsp) golden syrup

Power Level

Full (100%)

Serves 2

Linzer Torte

Method

1 Sieve the flour, salt and cinnamon together into a bowl and rub in the butter. Add the remaining dry ingredients before mixing together with the egg and egg yolk.
2 Cover and allow the pastry to rest in the refrigerator for 20–30 minutes.
3 Roll the pastry out and use it to line a 20cm (8in) round, flan dish. Trim and reserve the remaining pastry.
4 Line the flan with greaseproof paper and fill with baking beans. Cook the pastry case for 3–4 (5–6) minutes, turning every minute. Remove the paper and beans and cook for a further 2 (3) minutes.
5 Fill the flan case with raspberries and sprinkle with the sugar. Roll out the remaining pastry and make a lattice across the top of the flan.
6 Cook the flan for 8–10 (10–12) minutes, turning every 2 minutes until the lattice is cooked (it will not brown and crisp as in a conventional oven).
7 Allow the flan to cool. Meanwhile warm the redcurrant jelly in the microwave for 15 (30) seconds then brush the glaze over the lattice. Serve cold with cream.

Ingredients

For the pastry
200g (8oz) plain flour
pinch of salt
pinch of cinnamon
100g (4oz) butter
100g (4oz) caster sugar
grated rind of 1 lemon
65g (2½oz) unblanched almonds, ground
1 egg
1 egg yolk

For the filling
400g (1lb) raspberries
75–100g (3–4oz) caster sugar
2 15ml (tbsp) redcurrant jelly, for glazing

Power Level

Full (100%)

Serves 6–8

Cakes and Biscuits

Home made cakes can be cooked in the microwave most successfully with a good light texture. They do not brown as when baking in a conventional oven, but chocolate or coffee cakes or gingerbreads are 'self coloured' anyway and there is much to be said for them being cooked so quickly. Prepared and frozen icing for decoration can be quickly thawed in the microwave and chocolate for a topping can be melted in 1–2 minutes, so it really is possible to bake a home-made cake or gateau in next to no time for that unexpected guest.

Any suitable container including paper may be used for cooking cakes, but we have found that straight sided ones give good results and a better shape. The container may be lined with lightly greased greaseproof paper or lined with clingwrap but do not sprinkle with flour as this will only result in a doughy crust being formed on the outside of the cooked cake. Make sure that the container is sufficiently large to allow for the mixture to rise and as a guide, normally only half fill the dish with mixture. Generally, the wetter the mixture, the better the result but cakes with a high proportion of fruit do not cook so well.

If during the cooking, the mixture should appear to rise unevenly, it will normally level out towards the end of the cooking period, but if in doubt, just turn the container approximately every 2 minutes. Overcooking causes dry, hard cakes so remove from the oven when they seem slightly moist on top. As a general rule, when the cake has risen completely, give it one minute more cooking. Although we have found it is not usually necessary, if the outside of the cake is set before the centre, it is possible to protect these outside edges by using smooth pieces of aluminium foil for the last few minutes of the cooking period (see 'Aluminium Foil' page 13). After cooking, allow the cake to stand for 10–15 minutes before removing it onto a cooling tray.

When thawing a large, frozen, cream cake, give it only ½–¾ minute microwave energy and then let it stand until completely thawed otherwise the cream may melt before the cake is completely thawed and it is better to allow individual cream cakes to thaw naturally. Other large cakes may be given 2–3 minutes in the microwave and then allow to stand for 5–10 minutes before serving. An individual cake, or a slice of cake requires only ¾–1¼ minutes depending on size and type. Do not allow frozen cakes to get hot when thawing as this may result in a dry cake. As soon as it feels warm, remove from the oven and allow it to stand or heat equalise. If it is not then completely thawed, just put it back into the oven for another minute.

Individual biscuits are not always successful, better results are from those mixtures which are cut into pieces after cooking. However, the few recipes included in this section are well worth trying and good results can be obtained.

Streusel Cake

Method

1 Lightly grease a 19cm (7½in) round deep dish and line the bottom with a circle of greased greaseproof paper.
2 Prepare the topping by beating together the butter and sugar. Add the other ingredients and mix until a fine crumb is obtained.
3 Cream the butter and the sugar for the cake until light and fluffy, then beat in the egg.
4 Add the flour and salt and milk. Beat the mixture thoroughly and spread evenly in the prepared dish.
5 Cook for 4–5 (6–7) minutes, or until the cake is just cooked and shrinking from the sides of the dish.
6 Sprinkle the topping over the cake immediately and cook for another 1½ minutes.
7 Allow to cool slightly then turn out onto a cooling rack.

Variation

For **Coffee Streusel** dissolve 1½–2 15ml (tbsp) instant coffee in a little hot water. Make the liquid up to 125ml (¼pt) with milk and continue as above, substituting the coffee/milk mixture for the milk.

Ingredients

75g (3oz) butter or margarine
150g (6oz) caster sugar
1 egg
150g (6oz) self-raising flour
pinch of salt
125ml (¼pt) milk

For the topping

25g (1oz) butter
75g (3oz) soft brown sugar
25g (1oz) self-raising flour
50g (2oz) walnuts, chopped
1 5ml (tsp) cinnamon

Power Level

Full (100%)

Cuts into approximately 8 pieces

Light Choc'n' Nut Cake

Method

1. Lightly grease a 19cm (7½in) round deep ovenware dish and line the bottom with a circle of greased greaseproof paper.
2. Rub the butter into the flour and drinking chocolate. Stir in the sugar and walnuts.
3. Mix to a soft consistency with the other ingredients. Spread the mixture evenly in the dish.
4. Cook for 6–7 (8–9) minutes. Allow to cool for about 10 minutes before turning out onto a cooling rack.
5. When cold decorate with rosettes of cream or butter icing and walnut halves.

Ingredients

100g (4oz) butter
175g (7oz) self-raising flour
25g (1oz) drinking chocolate
100g (4oz) caster sugar
50g (2oz) walnuts, chopped
2 eggs
1 5ml (tsp) vanilla essence
6 15ml (tbsp) milk
double cream or chocolate butter icing and walnuts, to decorate

Power Level

Full (100%)

* ★★★

Cuts into 6–8 portions.

Genoese Sponge

Method

1. Lightly grease a 19cm (7½in) round deep dish and line the bottom with greased greaseproof paper. Sift the flour twice.
2. Beat the sugar and eggs together until thick – approximately three times greater in volume – and very pale.
3. Melt the butter for 1 (1½) minutes in a small bowl in the microwave cooker.
4. Sift the flour over the eggs and sugar and pour the melted butter steadily down the side of the bowl into the mixture.
5. Fold the flour and butter into the eggs until all the ingredients are well mixed together.
6. Spoon the mixture gently into the prepared dish and cook for 5½–6 (6½–7) minutes. The mixture rises during cooking but falls back to a height of about 5cm (2in).
7. Cool for 10 minutes then turn onto a cooling rack. Fill with jam or use as required.

Ingredients

4 eggs
100g (4oz) caster sugar
50g (2oz) butter
100g (4oz) plain flour

Power Level

Full (100%)

* ★★★

Cuts into approximately 8 pieces

Sultana Cake

Method

1 Lightly grease a 19cm (7½in) round deep dish and line the bottom with a circle of greased greaseproof paper.
2 Rub the butter into the flour and salt. Add the sugar and sultanas and mix well. Mix to a stiff dropping consistency with the eggs, lemon juice and milk.
3 Spread the mixture in the dish. Cook for 5½–6½ (6½–7½) minutes then allow to cool slightly before turning out on to a wire cooling rack. Brush with apricot glaze if required.

Ingredients

100g (4oz) butter
200g (8oz) self-raising flour
pinch of salt
100g (4oz) soft dark brown sugar
100–125g (4–5oz) sultanas
2 eggs, beaten
dash of lemon juice
6 15ml (tbsp) milk
apricot glaze (see page 64)

Power Level

Full (100%)

✱✳✳✳

Cuts into approximately
8 pieces

Chocolate Refrigerator Cake

Method

1 Break up the chocolate and put the pieces in a small bowl with the butter. Melt in the microwave for 2–3 (3–4) minutes. Mix well.
2 Beat the eggs with the sugar until thick and foamy. Gradually add the chocolate mixture, beating well. Add rum essence.
3 Break the biscuits into small pieces but do not crush completely. Carefully fold into the chocolate mixture.
4 Spoon the mixture into a 15cm (6in) loose bottomed cake tin. Press down firmly and chill in the refrigerator overnight.

Ingredients

200g (8oz) plain chocolate
200g (8oz) butter
2 eggs
25g (1oz) caster sugar
200g (8oz) digestive biscuits
1 5ml (tsp) rum essence

Power Level

Full (100%)

Cuts into 10–12 wedges

5 Remove the cake from the tin and decorate as desired before servi

Chocolate Oaties

Method

1 Melt the chocolate for 1 (1½) minutes. Cream the butter and the sugar. Beat in the eggs and cooled chocolate.
2 Sieve the salt, flour and baking powder together and add to the mixture.
3 Stir in the rest of the ingredients. Beat well.
4 Place in walnut-sized pieces on the glass tray, about 16 (8) at a time. Cook for 3 minutes.

Ingredients

100g (4oz) plain chocolate
100g (4oz) butter
150g (6oz) brown sugar
2 eggs
1 5ml (tsp) salt
100g (4oz) plain flour
1 5ml (tsp) baking powder
75g (3oz) walnuts, chopped

Power Level

Full (100%)

Makes about 60

150g (6oz) rolled oats
2 5ml (tsp) vanilla essence

Shortbread

Method

1. Line a shallow 17.5cm (7in) dish with cling wrap.
2. Mix the flour, ground rice and salt in a large mixing bowl. Rub the butter into the flour mixture until it resembles fine breadcrumbs.
3. Stir in the sugar then bring the mixture together with the palm of the hand.
4. Press the mixture into the prepared dish and smooth over with a palette knife. Mark into 8 and prick the shortbread thoroughly with a fork.
5. Cook for 3–4 (5–6) minutes, giving ¼ turn every minute.
6. Sprinkle with caster sugar, cool slightly then cut into pieces. Turn out and leave to cool on a cooling rack.

Ingredients

125g (5oz) plain flour
25g (1oz) ground rice
pinch of salt
100g (4oz) butter
50g (2oz) caster sugar

Power Level

Full (100%)

★✷✷✷

Cuts into 8 pieces

Variation

For **Wholemeal Shortbread** use:

75g (3oz) plain flour   pinch of salt
75g (3oz) wholemeal flour   125g (5oz) butter
50g (2oz) ground rice   25g (1oz) caster sugar

Make up and cook as above.

Florentine Flapjacks

Method

1. Line a 20cm (8in) round flan dish with cling wrap.
2. Melt the butter and syrup, for 1½ (2) minutes. Stir in all the other ingredients, except the chocolate. Mix well.
3. Press the mixture smoothly over the base of the dish. Cook on 50% for 6 (8) minutes, turning every 2 minutes.
4. Cool slightly then mark into 10–12 wedges.
5. Melt the chocolate, in a separate bowl, for 2–3 (4–5) minutes on 50%. Stir and spread over the flapjacks.
6. Mark into wedges and cut when nearly cold.

Ingredients

75g (3oz) butter
3 15ml (tbsp) golden syrup
100g (4oz) rolled oats
25g (1oz) demerara sugar
25g (1oz) mixed peel
25g (1oz) glacé cherries, chopped
25g (1oz) walnuts, chopped
100g (4oz) chocolate

Power Level

50%

Cuts into 10–12 wedges

Preserves

There are many advantages of making chutneys, relishes, jams and marmalade in the microwave cooker. Apart from the fact that preserves can be made quickly with very little fuss or bother, the flavour is enhanced and, particularly important with jams and marmalades, a very good colour is retained. You will find that the kitchen remains free of smells and cooler too. It really is possible to make just 1 or 2 pots of jam or chutney without the worry of food burning or sticking onto the base of the cooking container.

Best results are obtained with fresh fruit with a high pectin content, e.g. citrus fruits, gooseberries and blackcurrants. Fruit low in pectin, e.g. strawberries and apricots should have citric acid, lemon juice or commercial pectin added. Jams and marmalades should be tested for setting point in the conventional way, by pouring a little onto a saucer and leaving it for a few minutes. If the skin formed on the top wrinkles when touched, then setting point has been reached. Alternatively, a sugar thermometer can be used when the temperature should register 105°C (220°F) although some fruits may require a degree or two higher than this to obtain a better set. The sugar thermometer must not be left in the microwave when in use, unless it has been specially designed for use in the microwave oven. Use a 3 litre (6 pint) bowl or large heat resistant dish for cooking your preserves, leaving enough room for expansion when they boil.

After cooking, the glass jars can be sterilized by pouring a little water into each and heating in the microwave until the water boils rapidly. Drain the jars and pour in the preserves. Top with waxed discs immediately and when completely cold, cover with cellophane tops and label.

Three Fruit Marmalade

Method

1 Wash, dry and halve the fruit. Squeeze the juice and keep on one side.
2 Remove the pith and pips from the fruit skins and tie in a piece of muslin. Shred the peel according to preference, fine, medium or coarse.
3 Place juice and peel in a large glass bowl with the bag of pith and pips. Add 250ml (½pt) of the water and stand for 1 hour. Remove the bag.
4 Add the rest of the boiling water. Cover with cling wrap and cook for 20–30 (30–40) minutes, depending upon the thickness of the peel.
5 Add the sugar, stirring thoroughly. Cook for 25–30 (40–45) minutes, until setting point is reached, stirring every 5 minutes.
6 Allow the marmalade to stand for 20–30 minutes then stir. Pot, seal and label.

Ingredients

2 large lemons
2 grapefruit
2 oranges
750ml (1½pt) boiling water
2kg (4lb) preserving sugar

Power Level

Full (100%)

Makes about 2½–3kg (5–6lb)

Note

A clean 'J' cloth can be used in place of muslin when necessary.

Ginger Marmalade

Method

1 Wash the apples but DO NOT PEEL. Slice them and put in a large glass bowl.
2 Bruise the ginger by hitting it with a rolling pin. Tie in a small piece of muslin then add to the apples.
3 Add the water, cover with cling wrap and cook for 10 (12) minutes. Remove the ginger.
4 Press the apples through a sieve lined with muslin, to extract all the juice. (This quantity normally produces 500ml (1pt) of juice).
5 Add the sugar and preserved ginger to the juice. Cook for 25 (50) minutes, or until setting point is reached, stirring every 5 minutes.
6 Allow to cool for 20–30 minutes then pour into warmed jars. Seal and label.

Note

A clean 'J' cloth can be used in place of muslin when necessary.

Ingredients

½kg (1lb) cooking apples
7g (¼oz) root ginger
250ml (½pt) water
½kg (1lb) preserving sugar
100g (4oz) preserved ginger, finely chopped

Power Level

Full (100%)

Makes about ¾kg (1½lb)

111

Strawberry Jam

Method

1 Place the strawberries in a large glass bowl. Sprinkle with citric acid and cook for 15 (20) minutes, or until soft.
2 Add the sugar and stir well. Cook the jam for 40 (60) minutes, or until setting point is reached. Stir every 10 minutes at the beginning of cooking and every 5 minutes towards the end of the time.
3 Stand the jam for 20–30 minutes. Pour into warmed jars, seal and label.

Ingredients

1kg 600g (3½lb) strawberries, hulled and washed
15g (½oz) citric acid
1kg 300g (2¾lb) preserving sugar

Power Level
Full (100%)

Makes about 1½kg (3lb)

Apricot Jam

Method

1 Wash, halve and stone the apricots. Place in a large glass bowl with the water and citric acid.
  Cover with cling wrap, make 2 or 3 slits in the cling wrap then cook for 15 (20) minutes
2 Stir in the sugar. Cook for 45–50 (55–60) minutes, or until setting point is reached. Stir every 5 or 10 minutes.
3 Allow to stand for 20–30 minutes then pot, seal and label.

Ingredients

1kg 600g (3½lb) apricots
200ml (8fl oz) water
7g (¼oz) citric acid
2kg (4lb) preserving sugar

Power Level
Full (100%)

Makes about 2½kg (5lb)

Date and Apple Chutney

Method

1 Place all the ingredients together in a large bowl and cover with cling wrap.
2 Bring the mixture to the boil and cook until the desired consistency is reached, (approximately 30 (35) minutes.)
3 Pot, seal and label.

Ingredients

½kg (1lb) cooking apples, peeled, cored and sliced
½kg (1lb) dates, stoned and roughly chopped
100g (4oz) preserved ginger, chopped
200g (8oz) sultanas
200g (8oz) brown sugar
40g (1½oz) salt
500ml (1pt) malt vinegar

Power Level
Full (100%)

Makes about 2kg (4lb)

Hot 'n' Spicy Chutney

Method

1 Place the apples, onion, garlic, salt and sugar in a large bowl with the vinegar. Cover with cling wrap and cook for 10 (12) minutes.
2 Liquidise the mixture, return to the bowl and add the raisins.
3 Blend the spices with a little of the mixture. Stir into the chutney. Leave to stand overnight then pot, seal and label.

Ingredients

½kg (1lb) cooking apples, peeled, cored and sliced
1 large onion, chopped
1 clove garlic, finely chopped
25g (1oz) salt
200g (8oz) brown sugar
325ml (13fl oz) malt vinegar
200g (8oz) raisins
20g (¾oz) ground ginger
20g (¾oz) dried mustard
½ 5ml (tsp) cayenne pepper

Power Level

Full (100%)

Makes about 1kg (2lb)

Sweetcorn Relish

Method

1 Put the strands of saffron in the vinegar and leave it to turn yellow whilst preparing the vegetables.
2 Strain the vinegar into a large bowl, add the vegetables but not the sweetcorn. Cover with cling wrap and cook for 5 (6) minutes.
3 Add the sweetcorn, sugar and seasonings. Stir well and cook for 5 (6) minutes.
4 Blend the arrowroot with a little water then stir into the mixture. Cook for 5 (6) minutes, stir, cook for 3 (4) minutes, or until thickened. Cool slightly, pot, seal and label.

Ingredients

few strands of saffron
200ml (8fl oz) distilled malt vinegar
1 red pepper, deseeded and diced
1 green pepper, deseeded and diced
1 stick celery, finely chopped
1 onion, finely chopped
1 clove garlic, finely chopped
¾kg (1½lb) sweetcorn kernels, canned, fresh or frozen
200g (8oz) caster or granulated sugar
15g (½oz) salt
pinch each of mustard, mace, tarragon
2 15ml (tbsp) arrowroot

Power Level

Full (100%)

Makes about 1½kg (3lb)

Browning Dishes

With microwave browning dishes, you don't have to sacrifice the appearance of foods cooked to a golden brown. In just a few minutes you can prepare an entirely new range of dishes in your microwave cooker.

Browning dishes function in a similar way to frying pans or grills. With them, microwave cooking is capable of browning, grilling or searing food items such as beefburgers, steaks or chops. (Larger joints of meat and poultry brown themselves anyway during their longer cooking time).

Whether the browning dish is used as a skillet or a grill, it works in a similar way. Unlike the remaining surface of the glass ceramic dish which allows microwaves to pass through, the special coating on the underside of the browning dish absorbs microwaves when preheated. This makes the bottom surface of the preheated empty browning dish very hot. When foods are placed on to the hot surface, they brown, the same way as other foods do when added to a hot frying pan.

The temperature of the food, however, cools the browning dish, so food initially placed on the hot surface browns most attractively and when placed back into the oven, whilst the dish is browning the underside of the food, the microwaves are cooking the remainder of it. Foods should be turned over whilst there is still sufficient heat in the base to brown the second side.

Preheating

Preheat times vary with the size and shape of the browning dish, the output of the microwave cooker, the type and quantity of the food being cooked and the degree of browning required. Larger browning surfaces require up to 2 minutes longer preheat time than the smaller ones.

It is important to experiment a little when first using the browning dish to determine your personal preference. Try the minimum preheat time initially, but if you prefer browner meats, increase the time up to 6 minutes for the smaller dish and up to 8 minutes for the larger one. Preheat time for vegetables is about 3–5 (4–6) minutes, for breads about 2–4 (3–5) minutes and eggs 1–2 (1½–2½) minutes.

Placing a little oil or butter into the preheated dish immediately before adding the food, improves the browning of many foods, but in this case, preheat the browning dish for only about 4–6 (5–7) minutes.

Points to remember

1 The feet on the base of the browning dish prevent it coming into direct contact with the oven shelf or a kitchen work surface but care should be taken when it is hot to ensure that the dish is not placed on a surface which could be damaged by the heat from the underside.

2 The base of the browning dish becomes very hot, so the use of ovengloves is advisable when handling the dish. Whilst heating, the base of the dish will turn yellow but will return to its normal colour when cooled.

3 The browning dish should not be preheated for longer than 6–8 minutes. *It is not suitable for use in a conventional oven or on a hob.*

4 The dish will require preheating again when cooking a second batch of food. Remove all excess food and drippings and preheat the dish for about half the original preheat time.

5 Turn the food over whilst there is still sufficient heat in the surface for browning the second side, but serve the food with the browned, first side face up.

6 Foods should be thawed before placing on the hot surface as any ice crystals present may prevent browning although thinner foods, such as beefburgers or fish fingers thaw out quickly during the cooking period.

7 Whilst browning food, some smoke may be caused but this is quite normal. To help prevent splashings on to the oven interior cover the dish with the lid or kitchen paper towel.

8 The browning dish may be used as a casserole dish in the microwave cooker and is useful for sautéeing vegetables such as onions and mushrooms.

9 To increase browning of the underside, flatten or press the food with a spatula to provide more contact with the base of the dish before placing it back into the microwave cooker.

10 Do not attempt deep fat frying in the browning dish or microwave cooker as the temperature of the fat cannot be controlled.

11 The dish may be washed in a dishwasher or by hand but harsh abrasives must not be used as they may damage the special browning surface. Usually stubborn soilage can be softened by soaking the dish. If necessary afterwards, mild cleaners or a plastic scouring pad may be used.

12 The preheat and cooking times given in the 'Browning Dish Chart' are intended as a guide as times vary dependent on the size and shape of the dish, the output of the microwave cooker, the quantity of food being cooked and the degree of browning required. For those models with defrost control or variable power control, all preheating and cooking is carried out on full (100%).

Browning Dish Chart

Food and Amount	Preheat on full (100%)	Fat	First Side	Second Side
Steak, 1 150g (6oz)	6 (7) mins	15g (½oz) butter or 1 15ml (tbsp) oil	1½–2 (2–2½) mins	1½–2 (2–2½) mins
Pork chops, 2 200g (8oz)	5 (6) mins	15g (½oz) butter or 1 15ml (tbsp) oil	3 (4) mins	8–10 (10–12) mins
Beefburgers, 4 from frozen	6 (7) mins	15g (½oz) butter or 1 15ml (tbsp) oil	1½–2 (2–2½) mins	2–3 (3–4) mins
Bacon. 4 rashers	5 (6) mins	15g (½oz) butter or 1 15ml (tbsp) oil if required	1 (1½) mins	30 (60) secs
Chicken pieces 2 200g (8oz)	5 (6) mins	15g (½oz) butter or 1 15ml (tbsp) oil	5 (6) mins	3–5 (5–8) mins
Sausages, 4	5 (6) mins	15g (½oz) butter or 1 15ml (tbsp) oil		6–8 (8–12) mins turning 3–4 times
Fish Fingers 6, from frozen	5 (6) mins	1 5ml (tsp) oil if required	2 (2½) mins	1–2 (2–3) mins
French toast, 2 ½ slices	4 (5) mins	1 15ml (tbsp) oil	45 (60) secs	45 (60) secs
Pizza 17.5cm (7in) whole	2–3 (3–4) mins	15g (½oz) butter or 1 15ml (tbsp) oil	3–4 (5–6) mins	—

Recipes for Children

We have already said that the microwave cooker is so easy to operate that it can be used by any member of the family. Whether the few recipes contained within this section are cooked for the children or by the children, you will find them simple, quick and make ideal snacks for when they bring their friends home, or alternatively for the whole family!

Although it will undoubtedly be great fun for the children to try out these recipes for themselves, depending on their age and ability, it would be wise for them to check with an adult when first starting off.

Cheeseburgers

Method

1 Cook the beefburger on a piece of kitchen paper for 1 (1½) minutes, turn it over and cook for 30 (60) seconds.

2 Cut the roll in half and butter it. Put the beefburger in the roll, lay the cheese slice and tomato on top and then put the other half of the roll back.

3 Cook for another 30–45 (45–60) seconds.

Note

If you make 4 cheeseburgers at the same time cook the beefburgers for 1½–2 (2–2½) minutes, turn them over and cook for 1–1½ (1½–2) minutes. Reheat the finished cheeseburgers for 1½ (2) minutes.

Ingredients for each Cheeseburger

1 beefburger
1 bap or soft, round roll
butter, for the roll
1 cheese slice
1 slice tomato

Power Level
Full (100%)

*✱✱✱

Hot Dogs

Method

1 Heat the frankfurter on a piece of kitchen paper for 15–30 (30–45) seconds.
2 Cut the roll down one side and open it up. Butter the roll and put the frankfurter inside.
3 Reheat, in the microwave, for 15 (30) seconds.

Note

If you make 4 hot dogs at the same time heat the frankfurters for 1–1¼ (1½–2) minutes and then reheat the hot dogs for 1 (1½) minutes.

Ingredients for each Hot Dog
1 frankfurter sausage
1 soft, finger roll
butter, for the roll

Power Level
Full (100%)

✳✳✳✳

Double Deckers

Method

1 Put the chocolate on top of one of the biscuits and melt in the microwave for 30–45 (45–60) seconds. Spread the chocolate over the biscuit with a knife.
2 Put the marshmallow on top of the other biscuit and heat, in the microwave, for 15 (30) seconds. The marshmallow will 'puff up'.
3 To make the double decker, put the chocolate covered biscuit on top of the melted marshmallow. Leave to cool slightly before serving.

Ingredients for each Double Decker
1 square chocolate
2 digestive biscuits
1 marshmallow

Power Level
Full (100%)

Toffee Mallow Crunch

Method

1 Unwrap the toffees and put them in a big mixing bowl with the butter. Warm them in the microwave for 3 (4) minutes.
2 Stir the toffee mixture and add the marshmallows. Warm the mixture for another 2 (2½) minutes then stir again.
3 Pour about half the Rice Krispies into the mixture and stir well, making sure all the Krispies are covered with toffee. Add the rest of the Rice Krispies and do the same again.

Ingredients
100g (4oz) soft toffees
100g (4oz) butter
100g (4oz) marshmallows
125g (5oz) Rice Krispies

Power Level
Full (100%)

4 Press the mixture into some greased dishes and leave it to cool. Cut the crunch into squares. Alternatively, make small rock shapes from spoonfuls of the mixture on trays and leave to cool.

Strawberry Jelly Mousse

Method

1. Open the can of strawberries and drain the juice from the fruit by pouring it through a sieve, over a bowl.
2. Break the jelly into squares and put it in a 500ml (1pt) measuring jug. Melt in the microwave for 30–45 (45–60) seconds then stir well.
3. Add the juice from the strawberries and make the jelly up to 500ml (1pt) with cold water. Mix well.
4. Pour the jelly into a big bowl and leave in the fridge until nearly set. Pour the evaporated milk into the jelly and whisk them together.
5. Carefully stir in the strawberries and then pour the mousse into a clean mould or bowl and leave in the fridge until set.

Ingredients

1 298g (10oz) can strawberries
1 135g (4¾oz) strawberry jelly
1 small can evaporated milk

Power Level

Full (100%)

Serves 4–6

Cornflake Crisps

Method

1. Break the chocolate and place with the butter in a big mixing bowl and melt for 2–2½ (3–3½) minutes.
2. Add the golden syrup and the cocoa powder and stir the mixture well.
3. Add the cornflakes to the chocolate, a few at a time, and mix well to make sure that all the cornflakes are covered with chocolate.
4. Put spoonfuls of the mixture into paper cases and leave to set.

Ingredients

100g (4oz) chocolate
100g (4oz) butter
2 15ml (tbsp) golden syrup
1 15ml (tbsp) cocoa powder
125g (5oz) cornflakes

Power Level

Full (100%)

Variable Power Control Recipes

For those microwave cooker models with variable power control, the recipes in this section are intended as a guide to enable you to adapt some of your favourite more critical recipes, thereby making full use of the cooker's flexibility with slower cooking methods. Do not forget though, that all the information and techniques given in the introductory sections still apply. Of course you may still use all the other recipes given in the book which are cooked on full (100%) unless otherwise stated. You may find that after trying out the sample recipes in this section that you prefer the results obtained on variable power and therefore it would be advantageous to adapt some of the other recipes to be cooked in a similar manner. For example, after cooking 'Lamb Casserole with Leeks' on full (100%) and 30%, you might prefer to cook the 'Hungarian Goulash' given on page 81 in a similar manner, using the same settings – the choice is yours! With variable power control, your microwave cooker is flexible enough to fit in with all your family's needs and requirements.

Cheesy Spinach Flan

Method

1 Cook finely chopped onions in a small dish covered with cling film, for 1–2 minutes until soft.
2 Thaw spinach by heating on full (100%) for 4 minutes. Stand for 5 minutes.
3 Beat the cheese until smooth. Beat in the onion and egg yolks.
4 Drain the water from the spinach by pressing the spinach in a nylon sieve with the back of a wooden spoon.
5 Add the spinach to the cheese mixture and mix thoroughly, season.
6 Place the flan case on paper towels on the shelf of the microwave cooker.
7 Spoon the filling into the flan case. Bake on a lower setting (50%) for 4 minutes, turn, and stand for 5 minutes. Cook for a further 8 minutes or until filling is set.

Ingredients

1 17.5cm (7in) pre-cooked pastry flan case
1 onion, small, finely chopped
200g (8oz) frozen spinach
200g (8oz) cream cheese
2 egg yolks
salt and pepper

Note

Pastry cooked in the microwave cooker is best made with wholemeal flour to give it colour. Pastry should be prepared in the conventional way. Line a suitable dish with pastry, and fill with baking beans on kitchen paper. Cook for 3 minutes, turning every minute on full (100%), remove paper and beans and cook for a further 1–3 minutes for a 17.5–20cm (7–8in) flan ring.

Power Level

100% and 50%

* ***

Serves 4

Salmon with White Wine Sauce

Method

1 Wash cutlets, place in a dish and sprinkle with salt and pepper. Cover with cling wrap and cook for 10–12 minutes on 50%, turning once.
2 Make up 125ml (¼pt) of white wine sauce as directed using salmon stock. Cool sauce slightly.
3 While the sauce is cooling, reheat the salmon steaks in a serving dish for 2 minutes.
4 Stir egg yolk and cream into sauce. Check and adjust seasoning.
5 Pour the sauce over the salmon. Sprinkle with a few prepared shrimps and garnish with parsley and lemon butterflies.

Ingredients

2 175–200g (7–8oz) salmon cutlets
salt and pepper
125ml (¼pt) white wine sauce (see page 56)
1 egg yolk
3 15ml (tbsp) single cream
shrimps
parsley and lemon butterflies to garnish

Power Level

50%

Serves 2

Carbonnade of Beef

Method

1 Melt the butter in a large casserole dish on full (100%) for 1½ minutes. Add the onions and cook for 4 minutes.
2 Toss the meat in the seasoned flour.
3 Add the bacon to the onions, cook for 1 minute, add the meat, cook for 2 minutes.
4 Stir in the brown ale and sufficient stock to cover the meat. Add the seasonings, bouquet garni and mustard.
5 Cover and cook on a lower setting (70%) for 45–55 minutes, stirring occasionally.
6 Leave casserole to cool.
7 Remove bouquet garni, and adjust seasonings.
8 Blend the cornflour with a little of the cooking liquor and stir into the casserole.

Ingredients

50g (2oz) butter
3 large onions, thinly sliced
600g (1½lb) braising steak, cut into 2.5cm (1in) cubes
1 15ml (tbsp) seasoned flour
50g (2oz) streaky bacon, diced
250ml (½pt) brown ale
boiling stock
bouquet garni
salt and pepper
1 5ml (tsp) french mustard
15g (½oz) cornflour

Power Level

100% and 70%

Serves 4

9 Reheat on full (100%) for 3–4 minutes, stirring every 2 minutes until heated through and thickened.
10 Serve with crusty french bread.

Lamb Portugaise

Method

1 Wipe the lamb with a damp cloth. Spread the stuffing over the meat, roll up and tie securely with string.
2 Score the surface of the lamb with a sharp knife.
3 Place the lamb in a large shallow dish and 'open' roast on 70% setting for 15 minutes, giving the dish a half turn at the end of the cooking period.
4 Reduce to 30% setting and cook for a further 30–40 minutes until cooked through, leave to stand.
5 Melt the butter in a bowl for 1 minute on full (100%) and blend in the flour.
6 Add the stock, jelly, fruit juices and seasonings, gradually until well blended.
7 Cook the sauce for 5 minutes, stirring twice during the cooking time. Stir in the mint.

Ingredients

1½kg (3lb) loin of lamb, boned
walnut stuffing (see page 87)
25g (1oz) butter
25g (1oz) plain flour
250ml (½pt) stock
1 15ml (tbsp) redcurrant jelly
juice ½ lemon
juice ½ orange
salt and pepper
1 15ml (tbsp) mint, fresh chopped or dried

Power Level

70% and 30%

Serves 4–6

8 Slice the lamb, pour over a little of the sauce and serve the remainder separately.

Lamb Casserole with Leeks

Method

1 Arrange chops and leeks in a large, shallow casserole dish.

2 Mix the remaining ingredients together in a large bowl, heat on full (100%) for 4–5 minutes and pour over the chops and leeks.

3 Cook on full (100%) for 15 minutes, give the dish a half turn.

4 Reduce to 30% setting and cook for a further 20–30 minutes.

Ingredients

600g (1½lb) chops, middle or best end of neck
3 leeks, coarsely sliced
425g (15oz) can tomatoes
250ml (½pt) stock or water
1 15ml (tbsp) tomato purée
½ 5ml (tsp) dried oregano
2 5ml (tsp) dried mixed herbs
1 5ml (tsp) salt
freshly ground black pepper

Power Level

100% and 30%

✳✳✳✳

Serves 4–6

Microwave Steak and Kidney Pudding

Method

1 Grease a 750ml (1¾pt) pudding basin and line the base with a small circle of greased greaseproof paper.

2 Melt the lard in an ovenproof dish, toss the meat and onion in the seasoned flour and add to the lard, cover with cling wrap.

3 Cook for 3 minutes on full (100%), reduce to 60% setting and cook for a further 15 minutes, turning the dish every 5 minutes. Leave to stand for 5 minutes.

4 Whilst the meat is cooking make the pastry: mix together the flour, breadcrumbs, salt and suet, add the water and mix to a soft elastic dough.

5 Roll out a circle 1cm (⅜in) thick, cut a third from the pastry and put it to one side for the lid. Line the pudding basin with the large piece of pastry. Roll out the remaining pastry to a circle to fit the top of the pudding.

6 Place the meat into the lined pudding basin, damp the lid, place onto the pudding and seal the edges.

7 Wrap the pudding basin round with two long pieces of cling-film, stretched tightly across the top of the pudding, from top to bottom and left to right, place the pudding upside down in the microwave cooker and cook on full (100%) for 3 minutes.

Ingredients

Filling
25g (1oz) lard
400g (1lb) braising steak or prime stewing steak trimmed and cut into 1.5cm (½in) dice
2 lambs kidneys trimmed and cut into 1.5cm (½in) dice
1 onion, peeled and finely chopped
2 15ml (tbsp) seasoned flour

Pastry
150g (6oz) self-raising flour
75g (3oz) fresh white breadcrumbs
½ 5ml (tsp) salt
100g (4oz) shredded suet
125ml (5fl oz) cold water

Power Level

100% and 60%

Serves 6

8 Turn the pudding the right way up and snip the cling film away from the top of the pudding. Cook for 3 minutes, turn, cook for 3 minutes, turn and cook for a further 2 minutes.

9 Turn the pudding out and serve hot.

Curry Sauce

Method

1 Heat the milk and coconut together on full (100%) in a small dish for 1½ minutes. Stir, leave for 10 minutes, to infuse.
2 Melt the butter in a medium sized bowl for 1½–2 minutes on full (100%). Add the onion and apple and cook for 3 minutes.
3 Stir in curry powder and flour, mixing thoroughly. Cook on full (100%) for 1 minute.
4 Add the boiling stock gradually, beating well after each addition.
5 Strain the coconut milk into the sauce through a sieve. Add the remaining ingredients.
6 Bring to the boil on full (100%), stirring every 2 minutes.
7 Cook on a lower setting (30%) for 10–15 minutes to allow flavours to blend, stirring occasionally.
8 Use sauce as required.

Ingredients

125ml (¼pt) milk
25g (1oz) desiccated coconut
50g (2oz) butter
1 onion, chopped
1 apple, peeled and diced
1–2 15ml (tbsp) curry powder
2 15ml (tbsp) plain flour
500ml (1pt) boiling stock
2 15ml (tbsp) chutney
25g (1oz) sultanas
salt and pepper
pinch of cayenne pepper

Power Level

100% and 30%

Apple Bread Pudding

Method

1 Lightly grease a 20cm (8in) flan dish and line the base with greased greaseproof paper.
2 Place the bread in a large bowl, soak with the milk and beat thoroughly until smooth.
3 Add the butter, sugar, spice and egg and mix thoroughly.
4 Stir the dried fruit into the mixture.
5 Spoon the pudding into the prepared dish, and cook on 50% setting for 10 minutes. Rest for 5 minutes.
6 Peel, core and slice apple. Place apple slices on top of pudding while it is resting.
7 Give pudding a half turn and cook for a further 10 minutes.
8 Sprinkle with demerara sugar when cooked.

Ingredients

200g (8oz) bread, broken into small pieces
200ml (8fl oz) milk
25g (1oz) butter
50g (2oz) soft brown sugar
1 egg
2 5ml (tsp) mixed spice
50g (2oz) mixed peel
150g (6oz) mixed dried fruit including glacé cherries
1 cooking apple
demerara sugar

Power Level

50%

Cuts into 8 wedges

Rice Pudding

Method

1 Place all ingredients in a 1l (2pt) dish or bowl and stir.
2 Leave the dish uncovered and bring to boiling point on full (100%) for 7–10 minutes, stirring every 5 minutes.
3 Reduce to 60% setting and cook for 20–25 minutes, stirring every 5 minutes.
4 Sprinkle with ground nutmeg or when cold, decorate with mandarin oranges.

Ingredients

50g (2oz) pudding rice
25g (1oz) caster sugar
25g (1oz) butter
500ml (1pt) milk
1 5ml (tsp) ground nutmeg*
1 312g (11oz) can mandarin oranges*
(*Optional)

Power Level

100% and 60%

Serves 3–4

Fruit Cake

Method

1 Lightly grease a 19cm (7½in) round, deep dish and line the bottom with a circle of greased greaseproof paper.
2 In a large mixing bowl, mix together the eggs, treacle, sugar and oil. Gradually stir in the flour, salt and spice, and milk. Mix thoroughly and add the fruit and nuts.
3 Spread the mixture evenly in the dish. Cook in the microwave for 45–55 minutes on 30% setting, or until a skewer leaves the centre of the cake clean.
4 Allow the cake to rest before turning out onto a cooling rack.

Variation

100g (4oz) pitted, chopped dates could be added to give a heavier mixture if desired.

Note

If the skewer has only a little mixture on it when testing the cake, leave to stand for 5–10 minutes then retest. The residual heat in the cake will continue to cook the mixture for a time.

Ingredients

2 eggs
2 15ml (tbsp) black treacle
150g (6oz) dark soft brown sugar
65ml (2½fl oz) oil
150g (6oz) self-raising flour
½ 5ml (tsp) salt
1 5ml (tsp) mixed spice
100ml (4fl oz) milk
400g (1lb) mixed dried fruit
50g (2oz) glacé cherries, halved
50g (2oz) mixed peel
50g (2oz) chopped nuts

Power Level

30%

Yorkshire Parkin

Method

1 Line a 20cm (8in) diameter flan dish with cling wrap.
2 Place treacle, syrup and butter in a glass bowl on 50% setting for 4 minutes, stirring every 2 minutes.
3 Warm the milk on 50% setting for 1 minute, stir in the bicarbonate of soda.
4 Mix the flour, oats, sugar, ginger and salt, add the treacle mixture and the milk. Turn into the prepared dish.
5 Cook on 70% setting for 6–8 minutes, giving the dish a half turn halfway through the cooking period.
6 Leave to stand for 10 minutes before turning onto a cooling rack. When cold, cut into wedges.

Ingredients

125g (5oz) black treacle
100g (4oz) golden syrup
100g (4oz) butter
100ml (4fl oz) milk
½ 5ml (tsp) bicarbonate of soda
100g (4oz) plain flour
200g (8oz) rolled oats
25g (1oz) caster sugar
½ 5ml (tsp) ground ginger
pinch salt

Power Level

50% and 70%

Cuts into 8 wedges

Sticky Gingerbread

Method

1 Lightly grease a 20–22.5cm (8–9in) square dish and line bottom with greased greaseproof paper.
2 Melt the butter, treacle, sugar and marmalade together in a large bowl, on 50% setting for 6 minutes, stirring occasionally. Stand for 5 minutes.
3 Heat a little of the milk in the microwave cooker for 30 seconds, stir in the bicarbonate of soda and leave to dissolve.
4 Add the cold milk, bicarbonate solution and beaten eggs to the syrup mixture, stir well.
5 Stir in the dry ingredients and mix thoroughly.
6 Pour the mixture into the prepared dish. Cook on 70% setting for 10 minutes, turning once.
7 Cool slightly before turning onto a wire cooling rack.

Ingredients

100g (4oz) butter
200g (8oz) black treacle
75g (3oz) soft brown sugar
2 15ml (tbsp) orange marmalade
125ml (¼pt) cold milk
2 eggs, beaten
100g (4oz) self-raising flour
100g (4oz) wholemeal flour
2 5ml (tsp) ground ginger
1 5ml (tsp) mixed spice
½ 5ml (tsp) bicarbonate of soda

Power Level

50% and 70%

Cuts into 16 squares

Recipe Index

Recipe Index Continued

Thorn EMI Domestic Electrical Appliances Limited, New Lane, Havant, Hants PO9 2NH

A member of the THORN EMI Group   Part No. 81847

Printed in England by Staples Printers Kettering Limited, The George Press, Kettering Northamptonshire